MY CATS AND MYSELF

By the same author:

Recent Fiction
THE CANDLE-HOLDERS
THE BLACK SAMBO AFFAIR

Autobiography
YEARS IN A MIRROR

VAL GIELGUD

My Cats and Myself

A Fragment of Autobiography

DRAWINGS BY
RON CLARKE

London
MICHAEL JOSEPH

First published in Great Britain by MICHAEL JOSEPH LTD
52 Bedford Square, London, W.C.1
1972

7181 1027 7

Set in eleven on fourteen point Ehrhardt by Filmtype Services Limited and printed in Great Britain by Hollen Street Press on paper supplied by P. F. Bingham Ltd, and bound by James Burn at Esher, Surrey

For

JUDY, who took the photographs of our cats, and in affectionate memory of MERLIN II.

ILLUSTRATIONS

Part I
Strictly Personal

One

One spring morning in the year 1907 – or it might have been 1908 – a small boy was standing at the french window which gave upon the square backing his parents' house in South Kensington, London.

About this small boy there was nothing remarkable, except for his spectacles, which were steel-rimmed, and unusually large and round, and the spottiness of his complexion. The former he wore with neither discomfort nor complaint. He knew how essential they were to reading, his favourite occupation. Even when he went away from home to a private school in the country, and was promptly dubbed 'Beetle' by unamiable little playfellows, he had no objection. Indeed, having read his *Stalky & Co*, he felt rather flattered.

Acne on the other hand was his private cross, which he bore with neither resignation nor fortitude. He was not vain beyond the ordinary, but he did not care to be reminded daily, when he brushed his hair in front of the looking-glass, that he found the sight of his own skin faintly disgusting. However, it seemed that it could not be cured, and so must be endured.

I was that small and insignificant-looking boy. I was looking at the patch which led from the bottom of three iron steps beyond the french window across the square, and to the back of the houses on that square's opposite side. What I saw, coming along that path, was something which was to have a small but definite influence on the rest of my life. I saw for the first time a Siamese Cat. Cats of course I had seen before; several of them from time to time in that very square. But never before had I seen a cat with a body coloured palest *café-au-lait*, blue eyes in a mask of deepest chocolate with matching tail and paws. He, or more probably she – I never knew – was on a lead, and, tail held proudly in air, followed at the heels of a girl who must have been about fourteen, made conspicuous by hair that flamed red in the spring sunshine: a singular golden-red, which later I was always to associate with the Princess Flavia of Ruritania, and her lover Rudolf Rassendyll. She was exceptionally attractive. So much I realised. But at that period in my existence girls held no interest for me. (I might well have been a wiser and better man, if that disinterest had persisted.) I was only interested in the cat – and I believe it was at that moment I made up my mind that if ever, as I fully intended I should, I had a cat of my own, it should be a Siamese. It was one of the few determinations that I have been able to satisfy. . . .

I had never seen the girl before, and except in the far distance I was never to see her again. But I was sufficiently curious to want to know more about her. The difficulty was how to find out. In those days households which lived in South Kensington squares included domestic servants as a matter of course. That is the truth however improbable it may sound in this day and age. My parents might not be, and in fact were not, interested in their neighbours. Their servants – we had three, a cook, a housemaid, and a parlourmaid, not to mention my sister's nurse – were very much interested, and had their own means of satisfying curiosity. The cook, her name was Alice Stovold, was my special favourite. She made me free of her kitchen. She allowed me on occasion to inspect her black-beetle trap, which held for me a morbid fascination. She would always answer my questions, however embarrassing or fantastic, and probably laid the foundation-stone of my education. So almost automatically I asked her about the Girl with the Cat. It emerged that she lived with her parents on the side of the square opposite to ours; that the parents were wealthy – their house sported the embellishment of a greenhouse. The girl's name was Nara, and the peculiar pet on a lead was her Siamese Cat. And that was all I was ever to know of the first girl who, however indirectly, influenced my life.

I imagine that the reader's first reaction to this episode must be to wonder why on earth I did not proceed forthwith

B

to the acquiring of a cat of my own. It was true that, in contrast with Nara's, my parents were not wealthy, and I doubted if an appeal to their generosity, even added to the contents of my own money-box, would avail to secure anything so apparently exotic as a Siamese.

There were more formidable difficulties. The first was the fact that my dear mother was ailurophobe in the highest degree. The mere sight of a cat turned her faint. She knew at once, if a cat came into any room in which she was, even though she might not see it. This made the keeping of a cat as a house-pet by any of us children out of question. There was also my father, less vocal but proportionately more to be taken seriously. Despite his Polish blood, and his unusual talent as an amateur pianist, he was – and recognised himself to be – something of a 'Forsyte'. (It was he who first introduced me to *The Man of Property*, and in consequence was responsible, at a good many removes, for the radio adaptation of *The Forsyte Saga*, for which I was responsible some years before its more famous television equivalent was born or thought of. I fancy this would have amused him more than a little. Except for the fact that broadcasting had provided me with a safe and rewarding occupation, his views regarding the activities of the B.B.C. were hardly flattering!) As far as he was concerned the proper place for all animals – outside their original wild state – was behind the bars of a Zoo. Inside a private house they were both tiresome and unhygienic.

In spite of which it was his reading aloud to me of *The Cat that Walked by Himself* which first attracted me to all felines. The superb self-sufficiency of the Cat, waving his wild tail as he walked through the wet wild woods in Kipling's own illustration, was irresistible to a small boy, inclined to exalt a loneliness due largely to his distaste for other children of his own age. His fault, not theirs.

It was the habit of both my parents to read aloud to their children – a habit which today seems almost as incredible as their capacity to employ a domestic staff. With a certain sentimental regret I have to confess that I preferred my father's reading to my mother's. The latter – not unnaturally as she was Kate Terry's daughter and Ellen Terry's niece – was gifted with a naturally beautiful voice, and an instinctive sympathy with characterisation. This last I found sometimes embarrassing. Having been bred up in the best Victorian tradition my mother tended towards the reading of Scott and Dickens. The former I confess to my shame I found simply boring – I once threw a copy of *Ivanhoe* into the Humber in a fury of exasperation! While I was convinced of the merits of Dickens as a writer, my admiration was not increased by my mother's 'cockney', any more than my conviction of Scott's tedium was alleviated by her 'Scottish dialects'. Also the Terry lachrymal glands have always been weak. It is a weakness I share myself. Ellen used to 'dry' herself up during performance by bursting into uncontrollable tears. It is one of my brother John's advantages as an actor that he can cry visibly and unashamedly without exceptional effort. (His performance recently in *Home* was an outstanding example.) But for me the breaking of my mother's voice over an emotional passage was an embarrassment rather than an embellishment. I infinitely preferred my father's quiet, yet perfectly phrased, approach to his reading as both more agreeable and more effective. In particular as a reader of Kipling – and no author gains more by being read aloud – he was unmatched. I fancy that his inborn aptitude for music had more than a little to do with it.

So it was that *The Cat that Walked* walked into my consciousness and into my heart. I never met a cat to which I did not try to talk, or which I did not try – often without effect – to stroke. Self-sufficiency, elegance, and pride: the combination of these things came to seem to me infinitely worth while.

From time to time during the weeks that followed I saw Nara and her cat walking in the square. And there for the first time I saw in the flesh my *Princesse Lointaine* – the Unattainable Princess. I longed to speak to her. Even more I longed to stroke her cat. But I did not dare. And not so long afterwards I saw that the blinds were drawn in that house on the opposite side of the square, and I learned from Alice Stovold that one of Nara's parents had died, and that the family was moving away.

I never heard what became of Nara. I never saw her again. But I have often thought of her. If she still lives that wonderful red-gold-hair must be white. Of one thing I am certain; that there never crosses her mind the picture of a spectacled small boy, watching her from a distance with mingled adoration and apprehension, looking and longing. . . .

Many years were to pass before another chapter could be added to my Cat Saga. I went away to a private school near Godalming, where pets were not encouraged. I went thence to Rugby, where no self-respecting cat would choose to be found dead: an attitude of mind which only too often I shared, particularly on cross-country runs. I endured, and survived, a brief period as an officer-cadet designed for The Brigade of Guards – which had no animal mascot. I went to Oxford, where new and enchanting interests, including a variety of attractive girls, almost expunged the memory of Nara. I became, entirely to my discredit, and as the result of self-willed obstinacy, something of the family 'black sheep'. I left home. I lived for a few black months in unfurnished rooms at Chalk Farm, and later in a Knightsbridge flat, overlooking Harrods, as comfortless as it was diminutive.

However at long last the breach with my parents was healed. After brief and inglorious essays, as a salesman of typewriters and as one of the sub-editors of a so-called comic weekly paper, I secured from James Fagan the job of assistant stage-manager, and understudy to my brother John, in his production of *The Cherry Orchard* at the, then existing, Royalty Theatre. I knew only too well that I was not born to be an actor. I should have known as much by the fact that the putting on of make-up was always physically repugnant to me. But I had a job and a salary – both of sorts. And those were the days when it was not impossible even for a struggling actor to spend more time and money than he could afford in taking a girl to dance an evening away in a West End hotel.

I had two special partners in those days. One was a student at RADA; the other, daughter of a well-known singer in operetta, was one of my fellow-understudies in *The Cherry Orchard*. Both were charming girls, seeming the more charming to me because they never failed to encourage me to talk about myself. This self-revelation included my addiction to cats. And in 1928, to celebrate the publication of my first and completely forgotten novel *Black Gallantry*, B. and J. combined to present me with a Siamese kitten. I christened her, quite without any *arrière-pensée*, SEMIRAMIS after that fabled queen of the Assyrians who is reputed to have invented eunuchs. She was both pretty and affectionate, and I loved her very much.

Again domestic difficulties intervened. By this time I was again living at home, which for Semiramis implied necessary *purdah*. My mother, as always, was indulgent. So long as the cat was kept out of her sight, she could have what had once been the day-nursery of us children in which to run around. My brother John was not enthusiastic. To him – as years later another Siamese appeared to a visiting gas-man – Semiramis seemed just a wild animal, reasonably picturesque perhaps, but hypothetically dangerous. My sister on the other hand was, as ever, my staunch collaborator. All might have gone well but for the fact that Semiramis, like all her

kind, had and enjoyed making use of a singularly penetrating voice. It is the one attribute of Siamese to which exception can justifiably be taken. So Semiramis lifted up her voice and sang. But it was not a sound that appealed to my father's musical ear, even at a considerable distance. He heard; he disapproved; and he made no secret of that disapproval. The resulting situation was far from happy. Almost irresistible charm, which was my point of view, came into head-on collision with immoveable prejudice, which was my father's. For a time it seemed that a new, and more deeply-felt, domestic crisis might be the outcome. But just when the problem reached its most acute and distressing stage Semiramis solved it herself. She developed gastric flu, which in those days was almost always fatal to cats, and died far less ostentatiously than she had lived. And the sight and memory of that limp furry body, whose owner had become so precious to me, kept me faithful to recollection of her for several years.

In this context it is perhaps fair to record that during these years I was quite exceptionally busied with the harsh realities of earning a living. I abandoned my inglorious fumbling with the fringes of a career in the theatre, (just how inglorious is illustrated by the fact that its climax was reached with my engagement as an understudy in Edgar Wallace's famous melodrama *The Ringer*, which ran at Wyndham's Theatre for over a year!) after which it was with some relief that I forswore grease-paint in favour of the proof-sheets of the *Radio Times*, whose staff I joined owing to the friendly good nature of its Editor, Eric Maschwitz. So began what were to turn out as thirty-five years of continuous service with the British Broadcasting Corporation, and during the earliest of those years I had little time for cats.

I had realised instinctively that the cat, for all his self-sufficiency and independence, does not care for being treated as a casual plaything, a mere spare-time amusement. He is well aware of his position in any household in which he cares to take up his quarters. He perfectly knows his place – and that it is quite definitely above the salt.

There was accordingly no successor to Semiramis over the period during which I finally left South Kensington, to base my existence for the most part uncomfortably in Scarsdale

Villas, Earl's Court; in a tiny house almost immediately in the shadow of 'that great grey water-tower, that strikes the stars on Campden Hill'; and in a couple of rooms – with kitchen – in the old Adelphi Terrace above what were in those days the premises of the Savage Club. The principal advantage of the latter from my point of view was that they backed upon the flat at that time occupied by Eric Maschwitz, then married to Hermione Gingold. And I cherish to this day, and in my present home, a set of Foujita cat-prints, which 'Toni' gave me because, as she said, Eric could not appreciate them. Which reminds me that once in Paris I saw an original Foujita painting of two Siamese cats in profile, which I coveted on sight, and ever since have regretted that to possess it was utterly and completely beyond the range of the economically possible.

I am not pretending that during this period cats were altogether absent from life. A 'stray' could always be sure of a welcome, a meal, and a saucer of milk. In Scarsdale Villas a most attractive female silver-tabby came 'out of the everywhere', which was the desert of London, 'into here', which was our ground-floor sitting-room, and seemed inclined to make it her permanent home. But after some weeks, and much to my distress, the call of 'the everywhere' proved too strong, and she vanished as unobtrusively as she had arrived.

Apart from her most attractive appearance I remember little about her. But she taught me one thing which was an admirable corrective to a legend that had become established in my mind as a reality: the legend that the cat, both by instinct and choice, is a sadistic torturer of 'small deer'. It was that little silver-tabby who was the first cat whom I saw actually playing – and I choose the word deliberately – with a mouse. They were in the bathroom – how or why I have no idea – and were quite still about three feet apart, watching each other with supreme intensity. Unless the mouse moved the cat did not move. If the mouse stayed still so long that the 'game' had become boring, the cat would stretch out a paw, velvet-pawed and lightly touch the mouse so that the latter moved in turn. So it continued, while I watched and was fascinated. There was no hint of savagery, of 'nature red in tooth and claw'. For the cat the mouse was clearly and obviously just something that could move quickly and suddenly, like any clockwork toy. It was a case not of hunter and hunted, but of mutual interest and curiosity.

I have seen the truth of this confirmed since I came to live in the country, and have watched my present cats' attitudes towards voles, and moles, and field-mice. Primarily the cat is intrigued simply by movement as such. This may tempt him to wish closer acquaintance, and a spring – in which case, if the movement is a little slow or clumsy, the result may be tragedy. But a regularly well-fed cat seldom shows interest in the corpse. There is no evidence of sadistic delight in tearing or rending. The toy has unfortunately been broken, and will not work any more. That is all. And my wife has seen a mole, for instance, sitting up and seeming to fight back with tiny ineffectual paws, while facing what must have been to him the equivalent of what a sabre-toothed tiger would be to a man. It provoked no overt hostility in the cat, who continued to regard his tiny opponent with a curiosity which was almost indifference. If the mouse runs, having space in which to run, there will be a chase, and sometimes a killing. But the spring and the darting paw are designed to stop the chase, not to murder, and certainly not for the love of the latter. And any object will do: a hare lolloping across the lawn; a baby rabbit; another cat. Run – and the cat runs after. But that it plays torturously with its victims I resolutely deny. It is time that this particular balloon was exploded for good and all. That the cat is by nature a hunter is true enough. That he is a sadist is a grotesque libel, perpetuated, I can only imagine, by persons so mistaken as to prefer that common and unclean animal the dog . . .

But into that sempiternal dispute of cat-versus-dog I do not wish to enter. After all, and in spite of *The Cat that Walked* Rudyard Kipling preferred dogs. And who am I to disagree with him?

Between the front doorstep of that house on Campden Hill and the street there was a small patch of earth which must at some time have been considered as a possible flower-bed. In fact I seem to remember that for short intervals during my occupation it supported a few wilting hyacinths. When in the fulness of time I left what could more accurately have been described as one of a row of Victorian workmen's cottages than a house, there was also left in that patch of earth a small stone inscribed simply: BRONX, a Good Cat.

(There was perhaps a certain irony in that fact that little more than a stone's throw from that scruffy little house stood Moray Lodge, a noble pile standing in its own grounds, which had belonged to my grandfather Arthur Lewis, a haberdashery tycoon of the nineties. My mother remembered Moray Lodge well and with much affection, cherishing numbers of yellowing photographs of herself and her sisters, always with a horse, or a horse-and-trap in the background.)

Bronx was a ginger tom of great amiability and enormous dignity. He was equally unmoved by the comparative squalor of the neighbourhood, and the behaviour of that neighbourhood's 'strays' which tended to be hostile. He disregarded them loftily and went his own way. But for the most part he spent his time at full length on a window-sill or a wall at the back of the house, his coat aflame in the sunshine, and an expression on his face which I interpreted as one of quizzically surprised disapproval of the Passing Show. Unfortunately a petrol-pump station came to be installed on the corner of the street almost facing our house. For some reason this symptom of the blessings of modern civilisation proved to have a fatal fascination for Bronx. He would sit in the middle of the street, washing himself meditatively, and watch the cars as they manoeuvred into position at the pumps. And one day a lorry swung round the corner too fast, and Bronx failed to jump clear.

I have often wondered if that little stone is still standing in that patch of earth. But I have never had the nerve to go and see. It is long odds that as a result of some Local Building Improvement Scheme the house itself exists no longer.

Two

Bronx, as I have said, was essentially an amiable and good-natured cat. He proved it in the first instance by adopting no sort of grievance when, shortly after he came to us as a kitten, I felt constrained to have him 'altered'. I do not care to think what might have been the consequences had the 'permissive society' then been in fashionable existence. Bronx took it in his stride, for all that his figure was to an extent spoiled, and his natural force inevitably abated. Presumably common sense came to his aid, and he found himself prepared to settle for regular meals, a warm bed, and a great deal of affectionate appreciation. I feel it is also possible that, as a result of his disability, he was able to feel a certain superiority to the average tom-cat of the neighbourhood, who, like the average child of the neighbourhood, tended to be underfed, aggressive, lean, split-eared and scar-faced, and generally subject to a definite *nostalgie de la boue*. In such a common herd Bronx moved with something of the arrogant certainty of a mediaeval monarch.

The second proof of his good nature was, considering his felinity, less comprehensible, and with a longer history behind it.

While I was still Eric Maschwitz's assistant on the *Radio Times*, he made an adaptation for broadcasting of Compton Mackenzie's famous novel *Carnival*. In a mild way it made radio history, being the first radio-dramatic production to play consecutively for more than two hours; and dealing in specific sequences with a wedding-night, child-birth, and adultery – none of them regarded in those days as suitable dishes to lay before the listening audience. I shared Maschwitz's admiration for Mackenzie. I belonged to the generation of schoolboys who were brought up on *Sinister Street*, as later generations were to enjoy and be mildly shocked by Arnold Lunn's *The Harrovians*, and Alec Waugh's *The Loom of Youth*. When at the beginning of 1929 – to my immense surprise and satisfaction – I was given the job of B.B.C. Productions Director, one of the first things I did was to set the wheels turning for a production of *Carnival*. It duly took place, and, though I say it, turned out a startling success. Compton Mackenzie himself was persuaded to come to Savoy Hill to read his own linking narrative, moving both the cast and himself to tears! We became friends, and the following Easter Maschwitz and I were invited to spend a few days on the island of Jethou, one of the various islands which 'Monty' – as by this time we were privileged to call him – has inhabited, being, as everyone knows a lover of islands as also a lover of cats.

At this time, he shared Jethou with no fewer than thirteen Siamese, who would sit all round the candle-lit room while we dined, Sylvia, the matriarch of the tribe, being the only one allowed to tread delicately between plates and candle-sticks. 'Monty' was writing his *Gallipoli Memories*, and simultaneously suffering agonies from sciatica. As a result, having to spend most of the day in bed, he was most unwilling to retire at night. So he would read aloud to us what he had written during the day – with all the vivid effectiveness of a born actor from a great theatrical family – and keep us talking till the sun rose. I found it agreeable to gulp some fresh air in those dawns in the little coppice, which was an azure mist of bluebells, behind the house. And I could be certain of meeting two or three of the Siamese on the prowl, or stretched out flat on low-hung branches, watching the rabbit runways. Though that wood was not wet, nor particularly wild, they looked supremely happy and superbly in the picture.

When in due course the time came for us to leave Jethou 'Monty' came out with a suggestion as agreeable to me as it was startling. Among his Siamese was the 'runt' of the last litter, and he was concerned about her. Sylvia had neglected her. Her brothers and sisters tended to bully her. Would I care to take her? I certainly would – and so LULU, for so she had been named after one of the principal characters in *Extraordinary Women*, exchanged the isolation, and the bluebells, of a Channel Island for the asphalt pavements and the grime of Campden Hill.

And Bronx actually made her welcome. This in itself was strange, for in my experience the introduction of a strange cat into a home where another has become used to being 'master of all he surveys' is liable to lead to battle, if not to murder or sudden death. Not only that. Lulu, for all her charm which was considerable, and her looks which were exquisite, seemed determined to do her best to live up to her original. I do not mean she was lesbian. But her lust was insatiable, and she imitated the Great Catherine of Russia in preferring to choose her lovers from the gutter.

But before launching herself into this epic of Lust among the Dustbins, Lulu was properly and respectably mated with a certificated pedigree Siamese tom. Having made the necessary preliminary enquiries, and paid a visit of reconnaissance to assure myself that the premises were clean and the environment agreeable, I duly delivered Lulu to an advertised cattery in a secluded corner of Richmond. The journey seemed endless, and being more than usually hard up I travelled by bus and Underground. But from station to cattery was quite a distance, and it was a very hot day. Also Lulu had taken a violent dislike to her travelling-carriage. Never before had she been caged behind a wire mesh. She complained accordingly in no uncertain terms and at the top of a voice as penetrating as had been poor Semiramis'. The natural result was that I was regarded by my fellow-travellers with the deepest suspicion as evidently torturing a cat, and was treated to appropriately snide comments.

More humiliating still was the fact that when delivery had been made, and the tom was introduced, Lulu's reaction was a mixture of contemptuous *hauteur* and repelling ferocity. On Campden Hill she had seemed perpetually on heat. In Richmond she gave the impression of indomitable frigidity. It was the best part of a week, and involved me in two more trips to the cattery before the union was consummated. And its result was only a single kitten. I called him DAFFODIL after the epicene Norwegian character out of *Extraordinary Women*, and, like his mother, he appeared determined to live up to his name. Daffodil 'undulated exquisitely'; even before 'alteration' he seemed sexless; of all the Siamese cats I have known Daffodil was the only one almost completely lacking in positive personality.

Lulu meanwhile had flung herself with joyous abandon into a succession of affairs with lovers of the lowest degree. Tabby, black, ginger, parti-coloured – it made no difference, so long as he was disreputable of appearance and possessed the required vitality. There was always one, there were usually several in the neighbourhood of the back door, clamant for Lulu's favours, and simultaneously on the look-out for scraps. It was like part of the background to one of those Russian novels which were so popular among intellectual undergraduates in the twenties: down-to-earth; rather horrible; quite fascinating.

In addition to all this – a factor in the situation which I found and still find touching – Lulu provided herself with a 'steady'. Lovers might and did come and go, but Scarface – as I christened him because he had a split ear and a great scar across his face which added ferocity to an appearance in every way deplorable – Scarface remained: faithful, undaunted by repeated rebuffs, and seemingly unmoved by the unashamed promiscuity displayed by the object of his affection. Whenever she became pregnant, which was frequently, Scarface would hang wretchedly outside the house, as nervous as any prospective father outside the door of a hospital ward. On these occasions Lulu spent most of her time in a maternity basket in the kitchen, and Scarface would leave horrendous scraps of food for her on that kitchen's window-sill.

It was during one of these pregnancies that Scarface, so it seemed to me, achieved the summit of possible devotion. Lulu was evidently having a difficult time with the births, and I went down to the kitchen in the middle of the night to make sure that she was as comfortable as possible.

As soon as I entered the room my nose told me that a

stranger was present. He was. He was Scarface, and Scarface was sitting beside Lulu's basket, kneading her distended belly gently with his fore-paws, helping kittens, almost certainly sired by some hated rival, into the world.

But the time was coming, and early in 1933 it came, when circumstances over which I had insufficient control forced me to leave Scarsdale Villas for Long Acre, as formerly I had left South Kensington for Scarsdale Villas. Those same circumstances forced me to leave a good deal behind me, including Lulu and Daffodil, and though I left them in the best possible and most affectionate hands. I do not know to this day how I managed what I felt was desertion in the highest degree.

Daffodil did not survive very long. As he lacked personality, so he lacked physical stamina. Lulu on the other hand lived to a ripe old age despite continuous sexual indulgence and kitten-bearing. (I was credibly informed that her final score of kittens was no less than eighty!) There must be quite a number of cats roaming the back-streets in the neighbourhood of Notting Hill with more than a single drop of Siamese blood in their veins, and voices to prove it!

The changes implied by the move to Long Acre were considerable. In the first place my new quarters were a flat not a house. To go on with the flat was at the top of four flights of wooden stairs. The block itself had no particularly good reputation. Built round about 1890 it had been favoured, so I was told, by a number of ladies of the town, and one was liable to visits at untimely hours, usually by sea-faring men, demanding brusquely why Daphne, or Lois, or it might be Joan, didn't live there any more! On the other hand its situation was capital from my point of view. I could walk to almost any West End theatre in five minutes, and to Broadcasting House in twelve. This last proved most useful during the Second German War, when I frequently had to make my way to a broadcasting studio through the *blitz*.

For hypothetical cats the outlook was dim if not grim. The flats' front door gave directly upon Long Acre, which, Sundays excepted, was a maelstrom of heavy carts, heavier lorries, and trampling boots: for cats surroundings simply suicidal. There was, however, a capital kitchen in my flat, and from it access to a fire-escape and neighbouring roofs. These in the long run proved attractive enough, the roofs being often Wet and certainly Wild. And the cat, while exigent, is also adaptable. So it was not long before, with a certain feeling of treachery, I replaced Lulu and Daffodil with two other Siamese: RUPERT of HENTZAU, and RUDOLF RASSENDYLL. They were a most welcome gift, but the giver had made the mistake of purchasing them from a fashionable West End Pet Shop. They turned out not only to be well-bred, but fatally over-bred. Indeed within forty-eight hours of his arrival Rudolf had broken two of his legs merely by jumping from the kitchen-table to the floor, and had to be put down. Rupert, as might have been expected, proved of sterner stuff, and made an excellent if slightly temperamental companion for quite a time. But one day he got out of my front door; allowed curiosity regarding the staircase to get the better of natural prudence; and made his way into the street. He never came back, and I only hope that he may have been granted a sudden and painless end, as anyone who stole him would almost certainly have shut him up in a cage . . .

Three

When I think back to those years in Long Acre before the War, it is always of HUGO that I think. Of all my Siamese cats he was the best-beloved, the most intelligent, the most companionable. His society was only to be compared with that of a dearly loved mistress. He slept – his choice not mine – not on but in my bed, warming my feet in the chilly beginnings of the night, and perking up his dark-brown head on the pillow beside me in the morning. I had learned my lesson from the Rudolf-Rupert tragedy, and went accordingly for Hugo to a country-breeder, who did not believe in treating Siamese as exotic hot-house growths, but gave his cats the run of a garden and plenty of open air. I cannot claim that Hugo was wealthy; hardly that he was wise; but he was blessedly healthy, and cast out his shoe over Long Acre in no uncertain manner.

He could be savagely jealous. One night a stray black kitten mewed piteously at my front door, and naturally was offered the hospitality of slightly warmed milk and a blanket. All hell promptly broke loose, and peace was only restored at the price of an emptied soda-water syphon and a quantity of blood from both my forearms! If, as happened occasionally, I went away from the flat for the week-end – needless to say I always arranged for Hugo to be visited and fed during my absence – his reception of me on my return was both chilling and enlightening. He would hear and recognise my footsteps on the wooden stairs, so that he was always immediately inside the front door when I entered. But as the door opened he would deliberately turn his back; trot down the corridor to the kitchen; jump up on to the table; and sit, hunched up, his back deliberately turned to me; and so remain for a night and a day, unforgiving and unapproachable. Then, having made his point only too clearly, he would suddenly relent, and I would find him crawling down between my sheets.

Our idyll – it was nothing less – was inevitably interrupted by the War. According to plans previously arranged my Department of the B.B.C. was evacuated to Evesham. Nothing and no one could have induced me to leave Hugo in Long Acre by himself – the more so when it is remembered that in 1939 the general expectation was that London would be devastated by fire from heaven during the first forty-eight hours of hostilities. I determined therefore that Hugo should accompany me to the country. I recall most vividly visiting Harrods to buy him a travelling-cage, and finding that great store almost empty of customers, while the pale-faced assistants stood around in helpless little groups with nothing to do, and nothing to which they could look forward – as one of them put it to me – but the end of their world.

I got what I wanted, at no mean price, and the following morning packed a protesting Hugo with the rest of my exiguous baggage into the back of a car in which one of the members of the B.B.C. Repertory Company, just newly-formed, had kindly offered to drive me to Evesham. The roads were crowded. The standard of driving was deplorable. And Hugo sang an *aria* of distaste for the whole business the whole way from London to Reading.

Fortunately both for me and for Hugo my companion-and-*chauffeuse* had a wealthy friend of distinction in the motor-car industry, who owned a charming house in the Thames Valley. We threw ourselves upon his mercy and hospitality for the night; and it was sitting on the staircase of his house and in the company of his house-party composed of various rich and distinguished individuals that I heard Mr Chamberlain's historic broadcast which told of the declaration of war against Hitler's Germany. It was a little odd, though in a sense it may have been significant, that most of the hearers were openly in tears. Hugo meanwhile had been accommodated in an enormous barn and left to his own devices, though I suspect that his evening meal was proportionately luxurious. Certainly on the following day he showed little enthusiasm for renewing our westward journey.

Safely arrived in Evesham we immediately found ourselves in trouble. Billeting accommodation had been found and allotted to me. But the family concerned, while prepared to accept me without any notable enthusiasm, drew the line at Hugo. When I said that 'he was only a cat' they retorted, probably with truth, that they had never seen a cat that looked like that! They added that he was ferocious, and could not possibly be house-trained. Being both exhausted and a trifle nervous after our long drive I promptly gave them back those lies in their teeth! The situation however remained distinctly strained, and it was not improved by the well-intended but inept efforts of our official billeting officer, who expressed sympathy with me and Hugo, while admitting that our unwilling hosts had the letter of the law on their side. In consequence he only succeeded in infuriating both parties.

Things showed no signs of improvement during the next few days. Hugo shared my room – he would only have been removed over my dead body! But the household was so obviously both worried and scared that I did not feel that I could with decency remain. In consequence Hugo became what I think must have been the first Siamese cat for whom a furnished house was specially leased. It had a pleasant garden, so he was quite happy. He could hardly have been expected to appreciate the resulting strain on my income. But this was soon eased when a couple of my colleagues, who also had been unhappy in their billets, joined me in the house and shared its running expenses.

The period of 'phoney war' came and went. As the winter of 1939 closed in it became more and more obvious that for the Drama Department to operate from a base almost entirely lacking in technical facilities – studios in particular – and with a company of actors whose talents and enthusiasms could not altogether compensate for small numbers and absence of possible recruitment was becoming sheerly impossible once the Higher Authorities had nerved themselves to admit that there might be a demand for radio drama other than 'Half-hour plays of Childrens' Hour type', which had been suggested seriously to us as our primary objective at Evesham.

Accordingly we were moved to Manchester, to make life burdensome to our North Regional colleagues, but also to enjoy the facilities of studios designed for broadcasting, and the luxury of cooperation with an admirable orchestra.

The move was by no means generally welcomed. A number of secretaries in particular seemed to have taken a good view both of the amenities of Evesham, and of certain of the local inhabitants. Some of them indeed went so far as to suggest that I had some sinister personal motive of my own in abetting the shift. While professionally speaking I welcomed it, personally I was by no means so sure. For what was to be done with Hugo? I could not take him with me. I was to be quartered in the Midland Hotel, and I very much doubted its extending a welcome to a cat. Apart from which I would as soon suggest that Her Majesty might live in Bethnal Green as a Siamese cat in Manchester. And I think my misgivings were justified when I record, as a matter of fact not prejudice, that during all the months I spent in Manchester I cannot remember working except by artificial light, or ever seeing sunshine between one black-out and another. Providentially the same warm heart and kind hands which had cheerfully adopted Lulu and Daffodil made themselves available to offer Hugo a home in London, so that in his turn he went to live in the shadow of the Water-Tower, and later in a basement-flat off Ladbroke Square. Both he and Lulu experienced the results of *blitz* at comparatively close quarters. Neither was hurt. Both emerged from a sorely shaken house, expressing in very certain Siamese language their opinion of Hitler and his *Luftwaffe*. Alas, during the grim months that followed, there materialised an enemy more deadly than any air-raid: an epidemic of gastric flu which cut down cats literally by the score, among whom Hugo was one. I mourned him sincerely and missed him dreadfully. It only remained for me to console myself as best I could with the thought that in my personal Paradise, which will certainly contain cats, I shall find Hugo willing and eager to share my plate of ambrosia and my cup of nectar. I know that he will appreciate both – and I flatter myself that he will be glad to see me.

Four

The war went on. I, but not the bulk of my Department, returned to London, so that I spent some of the most uncomfortable months of my life commuting between Manchester and London three times a week on an average, during a period when the journey took all of eight hours, and the trains never provided food, and seldom heating. There was also the grim query ever-present in mind as to what one might find at the other end – especially the London end. I still remember the shock I received when after an all-night and hungry journey I arrived at Broadcasting House to find it o'er-shadowed by a pillar of smoke, and all the windows of what had once been my office blown in. (Rather singularly that blast seemed to have dragged open the drawers of my desk, and then banged them shut again, as I found the drawers full of broken glass!) The smoke was caused by nothing more dramatic than a hit on an adjacent building in the basement of which a great quantity of margarine had apparently been stored. It smoked furiously and stank abominably.

On the other hand it was good to be back in the familiar surroundings of my Long Acre flat, with my books on their shelves and the Foujita cat-prints on the walls; good also to feel that something like the real work which we were supposed to do could be undertaken with some prospect of success, now that I was once more in personal touch with the West End theatre. My first two productions after my return consisted of selected scenes from Shakespeare. They were broadcast from the old St George's Hall – so soon to be bombed in a shell of rubble – with casts headed respectively by Henry Ainley and Leslie Banks.

Naturally I had hoped to be able to reclaim Hugo. But, as I have already related, Hugo had decided that if there was another world, it must be a better one. think of him always as a casualty of the *Blitz*, and no one, cat or human, could ask for a nobler epitaph . . .

It has been suggested to me, at this moment of reading, that the account is to an extent heartless; that it might be crudely defined as 'one damned cat after another': an exploitation of the passive feline by the unthinking human. This is, I suggest, an unreasonable, even an untenable point of view. By the mere nature of things the span of a cat's life is limited to between some thirteen and seventeen years. (I have heard owners boast proudly of their pets surviving as far as twenty, and even beyond. But I am inclined to think that such claims are analogous to those made sometimes for the length of time wine has been stored in a cellar – and even the finest vintage can be kept too long!) For the genuine cat-lover it is the companionship of cats in general, rather than ownership of one cat in particular, which is the important thing. And, much as I have grieved for several of my cats, and especially for Hugo, I have always found it necessary – certainly after a decent interval – to find a replacement. After all, so I understand, the one vital necessity in riding is promptly to get on again if you are thrown. That, by and large, life is a cruel and unfair business, must – alas – be accepted by poor humanity. We must make the best of it. And that implies, however unwilling, the acceptance of grief and loss. It is also perhaps worth while to remember that no less an authority than Ernest Thompson

Seton has laid it down that 'the life of a wild animal almost always has a tragic end'. And the Cat, being essentially Wild, whether he chooses for background the Wet Wild Woods or the Wet Wild Roofs, seems temperamentally averse from any peaceful and immobile senescence. In most cases, it would seem, the Cat prefers to 'die in his boots'. And while one may grieve for a cat, I feel it is something of an impertinence to pity him.

This is, however, no more than a digression, expressing a purely personal point of view: one which dog-lovers certainly would not dream of accepting . . .

Five

As I have already described, Lulu and Daffodil came to me as the result of my association with 'Monty' Mackenzie in the radio adaptation of his novel *Carnival.* In the same way MERLIN THE FIRST came to me as the result of my association with Dorothy L. Sayers – how firmly Dorothy always insisted on the inclusion of that 'L' in all billings and publicity! And to this day I have never known its full-length significance. Dorothy had paid me what was probably the finest professional compliment of my career by making it a *sine qua non* of her acceptance of the B.B.C.'s offer of a commission to write a twelve-play sequence on the Life of Our Lord for broadcasting that I should produce the plays. This resulted from the fact that in 1938 I had come across a Nativity Play, written by Dorothy in contemporary language and in largely contemporary terms. I had been immensely struck by it. I made the necessary approach to someone of whom I knew nothing apart from the fact that she had created Lord Peter Wimsey, and might be adjudged formidable accordingly. However, as things turned out, both the preliminary negotiations and the production went smoothly. So it was with extreme excitement, not unmingled with apprehension, that I approached the problems of *The Man Born to be King*. These were considerable. To begin with the scheme for the plays had originated, rather oddly, with the Children's Hour at Broadcasting House. My colleagues in that department were naturally not pleased to find the business of executive production snatched away from them. Then there were the troubles automatically arising from conditions of rehearsal in time of war. Each play – and all of them called for large casts and elaborate and vitally important crowd-scenes – had to go from first read-through to 'live' microphone production within forty-eight hours. And this period included no allowance for interruptions caused by *blitz*, which were by no means infrequent, and could not be ignored as we worked in a studio, formerly a cinema, close to Marble Arch, which was anything but bomb-proof, though partly subterranean.

Much – possibly too much – has already been written both by me and by others better qualified on the subject of the preliminaries to the production of *The Man Born to be King*. There were various people, old enough and worldly-wise enough to know better, who, without having had a glimpse of a single script, worked themselves into almost hysterical convulsions. The Press of course had a field-day. One daily journal, now happily and justifiably defunct, went so far as to head-line the B.B.C. – in those days so long before the arrival of the 'permissive society' regarded as the very citadel of the Puritan Establishment – as 'A Temple of Blasphemy'. Mr Robert Speaight, who was cast in the leading *rôle*, was subjected to a stream of virulent and vicious correspondence.

Fortunately the Corporation, represented by its – then – Religious Director Doctor James Welch, preserved its head and its sense of humour. Indeed Doctor Welch went so far as to bring up his own heavy guns in the shape of a wealth of ecclesiastical dignitaries, headed by the – then – Archbishop of York, who arrived unheralded at one of the first of my rehearsals, and remained cool and unmoved while I addressed my slightly awe-struck actors, adjuring them 'to come down out of their damned stained-glass windows, and to remember that they were supposed to be normally bloody-minded human beings!' The Lord's Day Observance Society was left to burst blood-vessels in furies of impotent rage; and journalists who had thought that for once they had caught their favourite whipping-boy in the shape of the B.B.C. very much on the wrong foot, ate their words, and, I hope, salved their consciences, by giving the actual productions quite remarkably favourable notices.

All of which may seem a long way from Merlin the First, who arrived in Long Acre one evening in a hat-box, swung on Dorothy L. Sayers' strong right forearm. He was in fact brought as a peace-offering. Dorothy and I, most unusually – for I have met no author who knew so well how to define the respective spheres of influence of author and producer – had had a difference of opinion at rehearsal. And at some time I must have told her how greatly I had been missing Hugo. Hence Merlin the First: a typical and lively tabby kitten of immense and vigorous personality, who promptly made himself at home on the top of my book-shelves, and was to become over several years a very dear and cherished companion.

According to Dorothy he was no ordinary cat. She assured me that his mother, whom she had known intimately in her Essex village, had been a genuine witch's black cat; and she pointed out that Merlin bore on his forehead the inverted W tabby marking, supposed to be the badge of his unholy tribe.

Although naturally and agreeably mischievous I never discovered Merlin engaged in any actual devilry. At the same time it is no more than the truth to say that I frequently got the impression that he saw more things than I did. I would be sitting reading in the evenings, and suddenly become aware that Merlin was crouching in a corner of my sitting-room, his fur staring, his hackles raised, his whole attention centred upon something to me invisible. It was an uncomfortable experience, and one for which I could find no explanation – though I sought it from a number of people who might be presumed to know about such things. Only Dorothy, when I told her, would smile knowingly, and ask me what I had expected.

Why – Merlin? In the first place it seemed to me only appropriate that the son of a witch's cat should be named after the most famous of wizards. But there was another reason.

Almost simultaneously with *The Man Born to be King* I found myself intimately engaged with another radio play-sequence which achieved a certain notoriety: *The Saviours* by Clemence Dane, who was both a neighbour of mine – she lived then in Tavistock Street, Covent Garden – and a very dear friend. The theme of her series was that of the hero who legendarily returns from time to time to save the country in its hours of need, and dealt among others with such famous figures as King Arthur, Alfred, Queen Elizabeth's Earl of Essex, Nelson, and – as I still think by a flash of inspiration –

The Unknown Soldier in Westminster Abbey.

Clemence Dane – whom I prefer to remember as 'Winifred' – and I worked in close intimacy on those scripts of *The Saviours*. On occasion I was even able to make acceptable suggestions for inclusion. Of these latter the only significant one, which I remain proud to have contributed, was that the various episodes of the series needed a linking character, who should carry the theme forward from one play to the next, and I put forward with all diffidence the notion that King Arthur's wizard adviser Merlin would admirably fill the bill. Winifred liked the idea, and, needless to say, vastly improved upon it. And so Merlin, played in actual production by Leon Quartermaine with his unequalled loveliness of voice, headed the cast of each of *The Saviours*. So Merlin was much in my mind at the time when Dorothy brought me her witch-tabby, and his name was as much a tribute to Winifred and to Leo Quartermaine, as it was to his own hypothetically diabolical attributes.

Unfortunately he possessed one habit, both essentially mundane and incurable. He loved to climb. And the only climbable furnishings of my flat were my book-cases. As I have written, his first action on release from his hat-box was to spring to the top of the nearest book-shelves, and from that height to look down with wide yellow eyes, quite evidently 'monarch of all he surveyed'.

Devoted as I am to cats, and immensely appreciative of the fact that to be happy a cat must be largely a law unto himself, I am also greatly attached to my books. (Possibly because reading has always been my favourite form of relaxation, and because I keep no book which I do not wish at some time or other to read again.) In consequence, while I could not find it in my heart to blame Merlin for his climbing instincts, I came to take an increasingly poor view of his claw-marks scored across the backs of volumes which might have little or no intrinsic value, but which I cherished none the less.

However, by and large Merlin the First and I settled down very happily together, and I retain, and always shall, the happiest recollections of our companionship. However an occasion arose when I was invited to spend a week-end with some friends of mine who had recently indulged themselves in the luxury of a cottage not far from Sevenoaks. As a rule this would simply have implied my making the necessary arrangements with my elderly Irish *bonne à tout faire*, who fortunately was devoted to all cats, and had been to mine in particular since the days of Hugo, for her to visit Merlin on the Saturday and Sunday, and make sure that he was neither hungry nor lonely. As it happened she was not available for some domestic reason, and my friends persuaded me, rather against my better judgement, that they would be delighted to include Merlin in their invitation. I therefore dug out Dorothy's original hat-box, which I had luckily preserved against any such emergency, and carried him with me. He settled down with what I might have suspected, but did not, was suspicious acquiescence, and made the journey with no sign of protest or disagreement.

My friends' cottage was pleasantly secluded, and its small garden included a number of trees. Within the first half-hour of his arrival Merlin had gone forth on an errand of exploration. This was only be be expected, and caused me no uneasiness. But the situation became embarrassing, and in due course acutely so, when I found that he had climbed the nearest tree, settled himself into a comfortable crotch some thirty feet from the ground, and could not be persuaded to come back to earth. All exhortation was without avail. He was not to be tempted by food, carefully selected and strategically placed. Like Marshall Macmahon, after the French attack on the Malakoff during the siege of Sebastopol in the Crimea,

Merlin was where he was, and there he proposed to remain. It took the combination of a stable-ladder and far more nerve than I usually possess to recover him. And the cottage door had hardly been opened the following morning before he was back in his tree, and singing his satisfaction to the sky.

The result was a thoroughly uncomfortable week-end, and at its close, when I was on the point of departure, my friends urged me to accept the inevitable, and to leave Merlin in an environment which was clearly far more to his taste than the roofs and confined quarters of Long Acre. It went sorely against the grain that I might go home without him. But I should have known that once a cat has made up his mind it is futile to kick against the pricks. Trees were for Merlin the First his 'very heaven'. I fought against the conclusion. I took him back to London, protesting all the way *à haute voix*. I took counsel with Dorothy, who shrugged her shoulders; and with Winifred, who shortly produced what looked like half a tree-trunk embedded in cement, which threatened the stability of my kitchen floor, and completely failed to satisfy Merlin as a substitute for the genuine article. Our association had been very effectively ruined, and after some weeks I felt obliged to write to my friends, and ask them if their offer of adoption still held good. It did. And Merlin left me for Sevenoaks with no apparent sign of regret.

If he is still alive, which I much doubt, he must by now be a very old cat. But I think of him from time to time as I saw him that day, his paws tucked under him in the crotch of the tree, apostrophising the sky, and – I can have little doubt – weaving some feline spell appropriate to that master of the black arts after whom he was originally named. I am glad to think that I was not so selfish as to refuse him his obvious happiness. I will not deny that I missed him a great deal.

Six

It may have been in some sort poetic justice that my acquiescence in Merlin the First's self-chosen exile was followed by one of the gloomiest periods of my life. My personal affairs were in a condition only to be described as complicated, unedifying, and from the economic point of view ridiculous. I also accepted the assignment of secondment – happily only temporary, though its eighteen months seemed endless – to the B.B.C. Television Service, which I disliked only a trifle less than it disliked me! The consequences were not happy. And while I was somewhat conscious of a reproachful gaze from the shade of Hugo I began seriously to think that my existence might be considerably alleviated by the society of another Siamese.

It was with this thought in the back of my mind that one day I had the good fortune to be invited to lunch by Valerie White and her most agreeable husband, who then were living in an attractive house in Strand-on-the-Green. (Rather oddly it had previously been occupied by another friend of mine in Geoffrey Household, author of that superlative 'thriller' *Rogue Male*, which contains one of my favourite fictional cats: 'Asmodeus', who provides the hero quite literally with the sinews necessary for his private war.)

Val White is not only a supremely good friend and a much under-rated actress. She is also a notable animal-lover, being the only individual I have known in this country who kept simultaneously several Tibetan sheepdogs, those charmingly fubsy animated hearth-rugs, and a mongoose as household pets. On the occasion I am thinking of she had, typically, offered bed and board to the cat of a friend who had been compelled by some domestic crisis to go abroad at short notice.

And so it was that for the first time I met a Burmese Cat in the flesh. He came. I saw. And I was immediately conquered. He had many of the enthralling attributes so generally to be found in a Siamese: the lithe elegance; the quick responsiveness; the glowing eyes – but green in the Burmese as opposed to the Siamese's darkening blue; the certainty of movement; the obviously intelligent appraisal of a new arrival. And I went home with the decision firmly implanted in my mind that if Hugo was to have a successor, that successor should be a Burmese – always supposing a Burmese could be procured.

This was not so easy as it sounds, or as it would be today. I laid eager and questing hands upon any literature I could find relating to Burmese Cats. There was not very much, and most of it was hardly enlightening.

To begin with the experts, as so often, revealed themselves at considerable odds, and occasionally in flat opposition to each other.

Even over the origin of the species Burmese the authorities could not manage to agree. According to one 'in 1930 a female brown foreign-type cat was taken from Burma to North America. She was most attractive and much admired. As no brown male was available she was mated with a Siamese, and from the resultant litter and carefully selected breeding, the Burmese Cat became a recognised breed in the United States of America. In 1947 a breeder imported from an American cattery the first pair seen in Britain . . .'

Contrariwise another expert writes: 'The breed was

introduced into the United States by an American doctor, who brought a pair back with him from India – not as sometimes stated from Burma. Whether the Burmese Cat has in fact any particular connection with Burma is a matter of opinion. Some cat-lovers maintain that it is the sacred animal of the Temple of Leo Tsun in that country. I have been unable to find any confirmation of this belief . . . There can however be no doubt at all about the breed's very close connection with the Siamese. They are of the same build, and very similar in general appearance . . .'

This last is of course true, except as regards colour – the Burmese being of a rich chestnut brown, shading to slightly lighter on chest and belly, and to slightly darker on mask and paws. It is also almost certainly true that the Burmese has as little connection with temple ceremonies as the Siamese has, except legendarily, with the Thailand Royal House.

Enquiry revealed the existence of a Burmese-cum-Siamese cattery in Yorkshire, and a close friend of mine was kind enough to shoulder the responsibility of choosing a kitten which should be despatched to me in London. This was duly accomplished, and my first sight of U-PUSS – he was so called because from my exiguous reading about matters Burmese I had gathered that all Burmese gentlemen preceded their names with a capital U, much as in this country most of us cheerfully, and probably without warrant, add Esq. to our names – was of a small bundle of dark brown fur tucked away in one corner of a large wire-meshed basket.

The porter – there were porters in those distant days! – clearly mistrusted U-Puss's appearance profoundly. He had never seen anything like him, and it seemed that he did not care for what he saw. I had to walk over most of King's Cross Station, and visit most of its administrative offices, before I was free to take my cat away with me. His temper, when he first reached Long Acre, had not been improved accordingly.

However he grew up to be a handsome and elegant and – Hugo always excepted – almost the best loved of my cats. He was lithe, long-legged, and essentially adventurous. Among the cats of my acquaintance U-Puss was the only one to take kindly to travel by motor-car. With the insurance of collar and lead – and no one should take a cat in a car without both – he would establish himself on the shelf immediately beneath the rear window. There he would lie during the journey, for the most part peacefully sleeping, but on occasion casting a baleful eye towards the next in the line of pursuing vehicles. This was during a period when it was fashionable among people for the most part old enough to know better to place stuffed replicas of animals, usually tigers or leopards, in the back windows of their cars: replicas whose eyes lit up in coordination with the application of the brakes. It was fascinating to observe the expressions on the faces of one's pursuers, as they realised that the cat which faced and glared at them was a real live creature. But for the most part I fancy, and hope, that they were frightened rather than hurt . . .

Among other odd enthusiasms I have an irredeemable addiction to watching the game of polo. So during the Season it was my habit to go consistently to Cowdray Park. As everyone who watches polo knows, there seem to be at least two dogs to every spectator on the ground. It gave me a certain perverse satisfaction to take U-Puss with me to Cowdray. With the insurance against accident of collar and lead he would ride on my shoulder when I walked down to the pony-lines, regarding with a superb mixture of amusement and contempt the reaction of various dogs as they saw or scented him: usually surprise, occasionally fear, low-pitched growling, or high-pitched yapping.

I shall never forget one occasion when I rashly put U-Puss on the ground in front of the Members' Stand. A poodle, evidently feeling that this was really too much of a bad thing, emerged from cover and charged *ventre à terre*. Next instant it was abundantly made clear that to the poodle a Burmese Cat was completely strange, barbarian, and hypothetically dangerous. The dog braked suddenly and violently with all four feet, and for one hideous moment I thought I should witness a perfectly harmless poodle, almost certainly the apple of his mistress' eye, turn inside out in a reaction of sheer horror! U-Puss was nover officially banned from Cowdray Park, but I fancy it must have been a close thing . . .

I fear that U-Puss was something of an exhibitionist. The back door of my flat opened on to an iron fire-escape, from which it was an easy jump on to a flat roof, which was overlooked across a narrow street by a tall block of offices, largely occupied by energetic and frequently decorative young ladies engaged on their employers' business. On days of sunshine U-Puss would make his way out on to that flat roof; stretch himself lazily; perform an elaborate toilet; and ultimately assume a studiedly elegant and relaxed attitude, clearly enjoying immensely the admiring glances and the vocal expressions of wonderment and satisfaction from the aforesaid young ladies, to whom a Burmese Cat was as strange as it had appeared to the Cowdray poodle. There can be few more attractive things in nature than the glossy chestnut-coloured sheen of a Burmese Cat, lying contentedly asprawl in sunshine.

Meanwhile I have to admit that there nagged unceasingly at the back of my mind a longing for another Siamese: a longing both qualified and intensified by the fact that I developed a feeling that U-Puss might be lonely. His general attitude towards other cats approximated to the motto of the Scots Guards: *Nemo me impune lacessit.* The average Long Acre stray was not only made unwelcome. He was liable to immediate and vigorous attack. His reception of a new comer to the household would obviously create problems.

However, about this time I was flattered by the invitation to become President of *a* – I must emphasise not *The* – Siamese Cat Club. And in that capacity I visited their annual show, which was held at Reading.

I feel that I should immediately place on record that, generally speaking, I take a poor view of cat shows. I feel that the exhibits are too often unhappy; that the exhibitors too often approximate in feeling and desire to those characters who have ruined Association Football by turning it into a hybrid of Big Business and Show-Biz, and to the 'shamateurs' of show-jumping; and that most of the visitors are merely moronic, knowing little about cats and caring less.

Let me hasten to add that at this particular show my wife

and I were welcomed most cordially, and entertained most hospitably, and that we both enjoyed ourselves. That enjoyment was intensified by the sight of a litter of kittens, which immediately took our fancy; so strongly indeed that we decided that in one of them we had found the ideal companion and playfellow for U-Puss. We persuaded ourselves that with a really young kitten, and with the – perhaps unreasonably accepted – notion of relationship between Burmese and Siamese, no untoward antagonism would eventuate.

We promptly christened him THAI-PUSS, in acknowledgement of his Thailand origin, excused ourselves to our hosts, and took the kitten back to London with us.

The consequences were not entirely happy. What might be called 'diplomatic relations' were established. Active warfare, certainly atomic warfare, was outlawed. But the friendship which we had hoped for and almost expected from our two products of south-eastern Asia did not materialise. It may have been that U-Puss, being dark brown all over, felt an automatic revulsion against Thai, who was dark brown only in patches. It may have been that each suspected the other of designs on the other's rations. Myself I am inclined to think that U-Puss who was a big strong cat, looked on Thai not so much as another cat but as a rather elaborate sort of toy which it amused him to make jump and run by dabbing at him with his paw. Thai would run and jump quite satisfactorily. But he did not like it. And there was established firmly somewhere in the back of his mind an instinct regarding the Burmese breed: smell, colour, and behaviour. To this there was to be a sequel later on.

Seven

Unfortunately the bullying – it could not fairly be otherwise described – of Thai by U-Puss was not to prove sufficient to satisfy the latter's strong instinct for the chase. One of the disadvantages of living in Long Acre was its proximity to Trafalgar Square, and the resulting size of its pigeon population. I fear that I have always considered the pigeon tiresome alive and disgusting dead, and the Long Acre pigeons did nothing towards persuading me to revise that opinion. They were noisy, quarrelsome, and greedy. They would sit continuously or in relays on the window-sills of my bedroom and sitting-room, fouling them odiously with their droppings.

U-Puss shared my distaste for such habits. I would frequently find him glaring through a window at one of these interlopers, whom he clearly considered invaders of his domain, with what I could only fancy to be an implacable hatred smouldering in his greenish-yellow eyes, and motionless but for the slight twitching of his tail. And if by mischance a window was left open, he would crawl out on to the ledge outside in hopeful pursuit.

One such occasion proved fatal. He went out through the open window of my bedroom one night and did not return. Continued calling, search of the immediate vicinity, the window naturally left open, all proved unavailing.

There followed an episode which even now I do not care to recall. I had always maintained excellent relations with our local neighbours, in particular with the porters of Covent Garden, whose strength, dexterity, good temper and unique sense of humour I had come greatly to admire over the years. In particular their attitude towards the *blitz* could only have been described as literally heroic.

When U-Puss went missing we naturally made every sort of enquiry in the vicinity, hoping that a cat of such unusual appearance might have attracted someone's attention. My wife indeed pinned a notice on the front door of our block of flats, with a description of U-puss, a plea for news of him, and the offer of a reward for his return. Two days later, when our hopes had almost faded, we found a message scrawled across our notice to the effect that our cat was in the possession of a porter at an address in Floral Street. Our hearts bounded, and we sat up for most of one night so as to be sure of appearing at the given address the first thing in the morning, when the work of the Garden begins. The porter was there – but no cat. He had never seen a cat of the sort described. He had never seen a cat of the sort described. He had not read our notice. He could only suggest that one of his mates must have written up his name 'as some sort of a joke'.

To lose U-Puss had been bad enough. This seemed to me to be twisting the knife in the would with a vengeance, and to this day I cannot find it in my heart to forgive whoever may have been the perpetrator of that particular 'joke' for what no doubt was to him no more than a quite unthinking piece of cruelty.

A few days later U-Puss's body was found lying in a small alley-way leading eastward from the Charing Cross Road. What exactly had happened to him we of course never discovered. Geography made it impossible that he might have fallen from the window-sill into the street and so perished in his pursuit of pigeons. My own theory, for which there was no sort of evidence, was that someone or other must have come across him; have imagined from his strange appearance that he might be of value; and had purloined him accordingly. U-Puss never took kindly to strangers, and both his teeth and claws were sharp. He may well have drawn blood from an abductor who handled him clumsily, and have as a result been thrown out into the street, or just escaped. From where his body was found it seemed likely to me that he had been trying to find his way back to Long Acre, but failed to reach his goal. It is only fair perhaps to add that I have loathed pigeons ever since, and that it took me some time before I could look again with friendly eyes upon neighbours, any one of whom might have murdered U-Puss as surely as though he had shot him through the head. Cruelty, even though it may be heedless rather than deliberate, is surely the unforgiveable among human vices.

Eight

In consequence of the U-Puss tragedy Thai-Puss remained, and was to remain for some time, undisputed monarch of all he surveyed. And it was not until we moved from London to live in Sussex, after my retirement from the B.B.C. in 1963, that any addition was made to our cat family, with one most important exception: MERLIN the SECOND. He qualified literally as 'the Cat that Came in from the Cold', having been rescued from under the wheels of a brewer's dray by my wife, and adopted by us forthwith largely because of his startling resemblance, even as a half-starved kitten, to Merlin the First: the same big yellow eyes; the same inverted W – the witch-mark – on his forehead; the same furry amiability of disposition so typical of the nicest kind of tabby. Thai received him with a good deal of suspicion. But not even a Siamese could quarrel with Merlin the Second, who proved to be by nature both an appeaser and a peace-maker, as will presently appear.

While Merlin the Second and Thai are sparring cautiously as a prelude to achieving a mutually satisfactory *modus vivendi*, it may not be out of place to recall a few of the cats which I have met on my travels abroad.

In the first place it is important to make the point – especially for the benefit of warm-hearted elderly English spinsters travelling abroad for the first time – that the foreign cat is nearly always a very different breed from that to which they have been accustomed and devoted: 'Pussy, who sits by the fire and singes'. I shall start with Italy. I have had some experience of Italian cats, in Rome, in Venice, and in Sicily. I would not for a moment blame anyone who, on first sight, concluded that the Italian cat is regarded less as a pet than as a regrettable necessity; that it is half-starved as a matter of course; that it lives a miserable life as a matter of habit.

This is rubbish – and it is more than time that the letters which from time to time flood the British Press with agonised tales of the brutality of Latins to Cats should be exposed as the product of warm hearts and soft heads. The Italian Cat is by breed far more susceptible to the Call of the Wild, far more lean, far more rangey, than his English equivalent. Admittedly he is tough. Like his compatriots he thoroughly enjoys his food, and makes no bones about the fact. No cat is sentimental. The Italian cat would despise the word, even if he could understand it. But while the Roman cat in the Colosseum may to some extent re-embody the cruelty and ferocity of the heyday of Imperial Rome as represented in the Circus, the Venetian cat, indistinguishable in appearance, lies sleepily in the sunshine, licking his paws, frequently on a newspaper provided by a hospitable Venetian housewife, and garnished with a toothsome selection of household scraps.

There is, or was until recently at any rate, a small triangle of green grass, bushes, and trees, close beside the approach to the Accademia Bridge. On any hot day one could be certain of seeing some half a dozen cats there, stretched out in and enjoying the sunshine, looking out upon their world, and seeing that it was good.

And there was a small square, unfashionable and consequently unfrequented by the baser breed of tourist, where the coffee and brandy cost roughly half the price of that demanded in the Piazza San Marco – if perhaps justified by its two competing orchestras – over which presided the improbable figure in marble of one of the heroes of the *Risorgimento*. (It is curious that people as susceptible to aesthetics as the Venetians should not have realised that wide Victorian-type trousers and a broad-brimmed hat cannot be realised happily in statue form.) Here, attached to a small and unpretentious *trattoria*, we made friends with a small and very pregnant silver-tabby, who moved nightly among the tables with the certitude of a veritable queen, accepting a tit-bit here, rejecting a tit-bit there, according to her own thinking and her own desire. I should have liked to have seen her kittens when her time came. . . .

There were also two cats with whom I became acquainted in Sicily. They lived in the lower half of a villa on the hillside above Taormina – a villa celebrated by the fact that it was for a time inhabited by D. H. Lawrence, who wrote several of his better poems there. Unfortunately my host, who rented the upper half of the villa, where he lived in an exaggerated pose of misanthropy behind a locked iron gate and a frieze of cactus shrubs, did not care for cats, and did not encourage their society. He seemed to prefer *gecchi*, which scuttled – to me in seeming sinister fashion – up and down his walls in the intervals of absorbing incredible numbers of the moths attracted by his candles; and even hornets, which frankly terrified me by their size and their rasping buzz. Those cats were as nearly as possible wild animals. Any British spinster might have been forgiven for mistaking them for pitiable victims of inhumanity. In fact they were as free as air, and to all appearance happy as the Sicilian days were long.

Personally I have never seen an Italian abuse a cat, kick a cat, or throw a stone at a cat. Enthusiasts of the R.S.P.C.A. should look for subjects a good deal nearer home.

I once lived for the greater part of a year in New York. It

is hardly surprising that in a city so blatantly devoted to concrete, asphalt, and the internal combustion engine, there should be little space or opportunity of gracious living for an animal so individual and self-contained as the cat. Yet here again I was fortunate.

I was lucky enough to get the loan from a friend of an apartment in Greenwich Village. (This was in the period before the Age of Hippies and Strip-Parlours.) It was perhaps typical that while the apartment was at the top of a four flight walk-up, and two of its rooms – in one of which I did my writing – were about the size of a large cupboard, it contained two bathrooms. But to my immense pleasure that tiny room, which saw the birth of my only good play *Iron Curtain*, and my only successful play *Party Manners*, looked out upon one of the few tiny areas of green grass offered by New York. And in that area there gambolled daily for my delectation a pair of cats which I believe to have been Russian Blues, though I could never get close enough to them to make certain. It was enough for me to be able to look on and enjoy from a distance. . . .

There is one footnote to my curiosity regarding cats abroad, which is on the grim side. In the early autumn of 1945 I was so lucky as to be included in a small party of English journalists, invited by the newly formed Polish Government to see what remained of the City of Warsaw, and to help to revise the generally accepted idea that the members of a largely communist government probably sported horns and a tail. Our party also included Storm Jameson, the distinguished novelist, Bernard Newman, author of several capital thrillers, and Mrs Cecil Chesterton. The latter caused us some embarrassment when in going up the steps of the Wawel, the famous citadel overlooking Cracow, she was literally 'let down' by the failure of an elastic band, and an intimate

Val Gielgud with Hugo

Thai-Puss

Val Gielgud with Thai-Puss

Minou

Kitty-Puss

garment of canary-yellow slid down over her shoes. I have no doubt that I turned scarlet, and looked every which way. But Mrs Chesterton was made of stern Victorian stuff. She made no comment; stepped calmly out of the chiffon; asked me to put it in my pocket, and keep it temporarily for her; and proceeded calmly on her way.

It was the only one of our experiences in Poland with even a faintly humorous side. To this day I recall the shock I felt when, flying from London to Berlin, I realised that across the whole of Germany eastward from the Dutch frontier no chimney smoked, and no train ran. Here was the ultimate Abomination of Desolation, not the less hideous because it was well deserved.

Warsaw was more hideous still, with its rubbled streets so pathetically coloured by innumerable make-shift booths selling flowers. Those flowers, and the occasional poor belongings rescued from what was left among the ruins of their houses, were all the Poles had to sell.

After a few days I noticed that while we had been in Warsaw I had not seen a single cat. It struck me as odd, and I put the problem directly to my bear-leader, an agreeable young woman from the Polish Radio, who had upset me a good deal the previous day by suddenly bursting into tears because she could not identify a single landmark in the quarter of the city she had known best to enable her to see where the house had stood in which she had been born and brought up.

She looked me very straight in the eyes. 'Cats?' she said simply. 'There are no cats in Warsaw now. They were all eaten during the Rising, while the Germans blew our fighters off the barricades, and the Russians waited beyond the Vistula and did nothing! We had to eat something.'

No comment seemed adequate. There was a starkly Spartan simplicity in her sentences, which I heard parallelled when one of our party suggested that it might be both common sense and poetic justice to draft in German prisoners to help to rebuild the city they had dynamited and fired. 'Germans?' came the retort from one of our Polish escorts. 'It is unthinkable that anyone apart from Poles should rebuild the Capital of Poland!'

And again there was no more to be said. Indeed the thing went too deep even for tears. And until we had exchanged Warsaw for Cracow I did not see a single cat.

I have never been in Africa, so the African cat is as far as I am concerned an unknown quantity – though I would insist that the cheetah, which – alas – I have only seen in captivity in an American Zoo, is the most hypothetically attractive of all the Cat Tribe.

I visited that Zoo, while spending some weeks in Central State College, Oklahoma, under the flattering, if misleading label of 'Artist in Residence', where I was supposed to lecture on the subject of the contemporary drama, and discovered to my pleasure that while my students were bored by Brecht, and unimpressed by Pinter, they were all passionately interested in every aspect of Shakespeare and Shakespearean production!

My wife and I were quartered in an extremely pleasant little bungalow on the outskirts of the College campus and almost immediately we were made aware of a Siamese cat who, rather improbably, was investigating the environs of our dust-bins. Clearly it was impossible to resign him to such ignoble activity. He was given food, and encouraged to come again. He responded with considerable alacrity, and before we left Oklahoma we cherished, among other pleasant memories, the recollection of what had had become almost a Cats' Club, which assembled nightly round and about our back door with hopes that I am glad to think were not falsified. . . .

My experience of Asia has been confined to a single day in Istanbul – a day both rainy and cold – where I got the impression that the Turkish cat is very much a reflection of his native owners: savage; a doughty fighter; by instinct xenophobic; of necessity unapproachable. I have been led to understand that of all cats the Turkish variety is the only one which swims. Looking, with a certain feel of disillusion, at The Golden Horn, I could well believe it.

(Just in case anyone might believe that I am exaggerating or romanticising the case of those Warsaw cats which I never saw, I add here a quotation from Theophile Gautier regarding the Paris cats, besieged in the French Capital by the Prussians in 1870–71.

Wrote Gautier: 'Soon the animals observed that man was regarding them in a strange manner, and that, under the pretext of caressing them, his hand was feeling them like the fingers of a butcher to ascertain the state of their *embonpoint*. More intellectual, and more suspicious than dogs, the cats were the first to understand, and adopted the greatest prudence in their new relations with humans.'

For some weeks, – indeed until the supply of them was exhausted – the cat found a regular place on the Parisians' Siege Menu at the price of 6 francs the pound, alongside the rat at 50 centimes – though there was a noticeable difference in price between 'brewery' and 'sewer' rats – and the camels and even the two celebrated elephants from *Le Jardin des Plantes*, Castor and Pollux.

Another Frenchman described dog as being 'fine, fresh, rosy, covered with very white fat, exhilarating to the appetite when well prepared', while an American professor wrote of the cats that 'they tasted something like the American grey squirrel, but tenderer and sweeter'. It is no wonder that in consequence they vanished from the Paris streets as seventy years later they were to vanish from the shattered ruins of Warsaw.)

Nine

I am tempted by these quotations to be led inevitably, and I hope easily, into some consideration of the Cat in Literature. From Baudelaire to Sir Compton Mackenzie there has always been sympathy apparent between cats and writers, and a shelf of books in my library contains many, all of them well-thumbed, relating to the cult of the Cat.

'Monty' Mackenzie – am I alone in finding it odd that this most approachable of men should have been christened Montague? – is of course as well known for his Comprehension of Cats as he is for his novels, his occupation of various islands, and his devotion to the cause of Scottish Nationalism. But among others – and the list is not comprehensive, while the choice of names included may seem invidious – Doris Lessing with *Particularly Cats*, Sir John Smyth V.C. with *Beloved Cats*, Olivia Manning with *Extra-ordinary Cats*, Miss Read with *Tiggy*, Marguerite Steen with *Little White King*, Paul Gallico with *The Silent Miaow*, have all written on the subject revealing after their different and individual fashions observation, perceptive sensitivity, affection, and above all enthusiasm.

It is unnecessary, but it would I feel be ungracious to make no mention of T. S. Eliot's *Old Possum's Book of Practical Cats*, or of the late Michael Joseph's acknowledged small classic *Charles*.

Personally, I would have a child as familiar with Kipling's

Cat That Walked by Himself and Beatrix Potter's *Tale of Tom Kitten*, as he or she inevitably is with *Alice in Wonderland*. (Both, of course, should be read aloud.)

What is the common factor which makes for the sympathy between writers and cats? I have often wondered, and now come up with an answer for what it may be worth.

At best the writer's Craft – I will not bedevil the issue by calling it Art – is a lonely business. It demands quiet, a modest degree of material comfort, and absence of interruption. At the same time the writer, being as a rule both sensitive and vain beyond the ordinary – or he would not be a writer – needs company and even an audience. Many of the writers I have met need an audience of appreciation as much as any actor.

It is this company, accompanied by absence of interruption, which I have found provided over the years by my cats. Either they sleep peacefully in an adjacent arm-chair, their tails curled endearingly across their noses; or they will couch amiably upon my knees, simultaneously regardless of the clatter of the typewriter, or of the fumes of my cigarette smoke. The cat is there. He does not comment or suggest improvements. He assuages loneliness, but he does not demand the reciprocation of attention. His attitude is that of one individualist to another. It is proportionately precious.

The cat is there; but he does not insist upon recognition that he is there. He seems to enjoy conversation, which must be one-sided – as was recognised by Hilaire Belloc. Hugo's only comment upon the writing of sensational fiction was occasionally to walk across my desk, flicking at carbons and ash-trays with a casually planted hind-leg. If I have been temporarily 'grassed' for word or phrase, I have been able to rely on a sociable interlude with one of my cats, always ready and available to break the tiresome spells of hopelessly improbable complications of plot, or of verbal constipation.

There is also the curious, and quite inexplicable, factor of *mystique*. I am not referring to the traditional communication supposed to exist between cats and the Powers of Darkness. I will not pretend that I really believed Dorothy Sayers when she talked, with all apparent seriousness, of 'Witches' Cats', nor that I believed that she was serious. None the less the tradition exists, and has been known to exist for more centuries than it is comfortable to count. The witch, with her broom-stick and black cat, may be no more than a nursery legend, an illustration in a child's picture-book, or one of the hoariest of jokes. But only four hundred years ago – no more than a moment in historical perspective – the witch was anything but a joke, as was proved by the fate of many poor, old, and often half-witted women, who were regarded with distrust by their neighbours, and perhaps for that very reason treated their cats with greater familiarity than was wise.

There are a number of reasons why the cat should have gained this suspect reputation: his turning of night into day together with his ability – now I understand questioned – to see in the dark; his individualism; his self-sufficiency, so often considered mere arrogance; the fact that he is chased on sight and principle by that amiably cheerful extrovert the dog, who, especially if combined with pipe, is well-known as the indispensable companion of every respectable Englishman; his fabled nine lives. There is the definition, in a mediaeval dictionary which says flatly: 'The Catte – an oncleane beaste', which must be about the nearest to flat libel to be attained even by a chronicler of the Middle Ages.

So as he walks down that long avenue which leads from the Past to the Present – tail proudly erect and every nerve at stretch to guard against sudden emergency – the Cat must feel himself flanked by a succession of ghosts of fiction

(Algernon Blackwood), demons of tradition (James Branch Cabell and H. H. Munro, better known as 'Saki'), improbable representatives of his own kind (Conan Doyle).

To the writer the Cat has proved both a boon and a blessing. And if their alliance had produced nothing more than the story of *Tobermory* it would have more than justified itself.

Shifting for a moment from the near-sublime to the almost-ridiculous, I have to confess that during my long periods of service and incarceration behind the concrete battlements of Broadcasting House I had only a single encounter with cats. They were not encouraged to form a recognised part of the Radio Establishment, though I often felt that during long arguments with colleagues in my office, and even longer Meetings – a word which every retired bureaucrat must recall with horror! – the presence of a cat, and particularly of a Siamese Cat would have gone far towards sweetening pills.

During the period while 'the battleship of Portland Place' was actually under construction, I was invited to go and look over it: a proceeding both wearisome, and, as it took place at night-time, not particularly revealing. However amongst all the confusion inseparable from all building operations – the dust, the inclined boards leading to nowhere in particular, the barrows, and the hammering, there suddenly appeared two cats, their eyes shining through the murk of what I was confidently assured would one day be revealed as one of the corridors on the fifth floor of the Studio Tower. (I could naturally have been expected to be individually interested, as the fifth and sixth floors of this Tower were designed to include my drama studios, from which so many plays went out on to the British air, until during one night of the *blitz* Broadcasting House became a target; and a bomb lay for some ten minutes unnoticed on that fifth floor before finally it exploded with tragic results for a Polish monitoring section, which was in temporary occupation.)

There is no record of the fate of the cats. But one of the engineers informed me that they had, as it were, grown up with the building. They had requisitioned quarters while the foundations were being laid, and had moved gradually upwards from floor to floor. He added that they were practically 'wild beasts', and quite unapproachable. . . .

Ten

Perhaps it is time to return to Long Acre, where Thai-Puss and Merlin the Second are sparring cautiously for position.

In actual fact Merlin, although saved by my wife from the equivalent of worse than death in Covent Garden, did not immediately enter our family circle. He was at first adopted by an Italian lady, the housekeeper of a denizen of one of the lower floors of our block, who had much of what the eighteenth century knew as 'bottom', but which in contemporary terms implied no more than a warm heart and a capacious bosom. To this bosom Merlin the Second found himself most warmly clasped. It may have been that he found the capaciousness excessive. In my opinion it is more likely that he took a poor view, being a determinedly English cat, of a diet largely composed of rice left-overs.

However that may be, he was soon almost daily to be first heard, and then seen, on the fire-escape outside our back door, mewing piteously for food and alternative society. It was a difficult situation, solved by the return of the Italian lady's mistress, who was quite firm on the subject of stray cats. And Merlin was brought back to us, hugged against that capacious bosom, and handed over to my wife who made no bones about her delight at his reappearance.

Thai's first reception of the newcomer could only be described as snobbish in the extreme. He pretended to ignore him – simply, to pretend that Merlin wasn't there. Thai slept on our bed, while Merlin was confined to a basket in the kitchen. Each morning Merlin would emerge, apparently smiling to the edge of his whiskers, purring loudly, and offering to kiss Thai on the tip of his aristocratic nose. At which approach Thai would shudder visibly down to the end of his tail.

However, possibly as the result of cause and effect, Thai seemed to take a more favourable view when Merlin left us temporarily for the necessary neutering operation. Thai appeared to miss him, and showed signs of welcome on his return.

When at last the time came for us to move from Long Acre to Barcombe, Sussex, and the furniture and books had been packed up accordingly, Thai suddenly decided that he would like to share Merlin's sleeping-quarters in the kitchen, and did so ever afterwards. After the slightly bullying superiority of attitude of U-Puss, Merlin must have seemed unbelievably more agreeable as a companion. Though, like U-Puss, a big cat, Merlin was amiable in disposition almost to a fault, besides being most comfortably furry and friendly.

En route to Wychwood, our destination in the country, Thai, in a basket on the back seat of the car, sang all the way as once Hugo had sung *en route* to Reading on that first day of the Second German War. Contrariwise Merlin, after the first few miles, went peacefully to sleep and so continued. Once arrived, we let them out to roam over the empty house and acquaint themselves with its advantages, and disadvantages; and then shut them in an empty bathroom with a notice on the door forbidding entrance to curious furniture-removers. Once released, they started exploring together, taking it in turns to lead. We showed them how to get in and out of the outside world by way of the lid of a coal-bin and the kitchen-window. Thai proceeded with immense and tentative caution. Merlin bounded away with chirruping sounds that encouraged us to think that he would settle easily into his new environment.

This proved happily to be the case with both cats, though to begin with Thai remained distinctly suspicious of his new surroundings, in particular for a reason shortly to be made clear.

Let no one aver that cats have no memories. As will appear when I come to record my acquisition, a considerable time later, of another Burmese, Thai made it abundantly clear that recollections of his treatment by U-Puss were still very vivid in his mind. Similarly Merlin, who, as I have emphasised, was the most gentle and friendly of cats, must have preserved memories of those heavy and mud-stained boots which must so often have been nearly fatal to him in the surroundings of Covent Garden. The only thing in the country which caused him apprehension was the sight and smell, probably both, of heavy boots, particularly the boots of our gardener, a fascinating old character of eighty-three, formerly a worker on the local railway, and now eking out his old-age pension by ‘gardening’ for two or three days in the week. His approach to the cats was perfectly civil, but it only needed the sound of his boots clumping on the surface of our modest drive to send Merlin into absolute panic, and frequently up the nearest tree in a dash for safety. (He had not Merlin the First’s passion for climbing, but clearly appreciated the value of leaves and branches as providing security and camouflage in emergency.)

Merlin soon came to enjoy country walking, and would trot happily behind his mistress on expeditions along lanes and over fields. But on one occasion, when she encountered a stranger in the neighbourhood who was wearing vasty wellingtons, Merlin bolted into the wide blue yonder, and after causing us the grimmest fears for his fate and future was ultimately found crouching in a field of cabbages, responding to our frantic calls with a combination of purring and piteous mews.

The move to Wychwood produced one curious and to me most interesting example of what Robert Ardrey has referred to as animals’ right of dominion over their own territory.

The house’s previous occupants had owned a black cat, a comparatively elderly lady, spayed, with glossy fur and quite beautiful green eyes. They were moving into quarters in Hove, where they felt that MINOU – that was the lady’s name – would neither be comfortable nor safe. In consequence they felt obliged, with much regret, to tell me that unless we were prepared to accept Minou, they would be compelled to have her ‘put down’.

This I could not contemplate – partly for her own sake, as Minou had been both welcoming and companionable while Judy was for a short time alone in the house during the preliminaries to the move, but even more because, without being unreasonably superstitious, I felt that to enter upon

ownership of a new house, and to cement that ownership, as it were, with the blood of a black cat, would be to ask for trouble and ill-luck in the biggest way! We therefore accepted Minou, and in due course brought her, Thai and Merlin the Second together, and waited to see what would happen.

It must be said for Thai and Merlin that their attitude was unexceptionable. Apparently realising that Minou was entitled to the privileges conferred by long-term occupation, they approached her with respect, and made the friendliest of overtures. But while Man may propose, Cats certainly will dispose. Minou not only stood upon her undoubted rights. She evinced active hostility to strangers within her territory. She laid back her ears. She snarled. She spat. I grew progressively afraid lest one day I might have to witness the fur flying in some battle to the death.

It remained for Thai to settle the matter out of hand. (I cannot say whether in his case he felt he was being victimised on grounds of colour prejudice!) After about a fortnight of consistent bloody-mindedness on the part of Minou, Thai suddenly decided that he had had enough. Minou might be a female. She was also – and this was long before the days of Women's Lib! – intolerable. He flew at her with clearly no holds barred. Then Minou made her fatal mistake. She turned and ran. And from that moment Thai, feeling that he had finally established the right to his territory, would not allow Minou so much as to put her nose inside the door of sitting-room, dining-room, or kitchen, without being immediately and fiercely assaulted.

It became necessary to establish Minou in a small lobby just inside the front door, with regular meals, a shelf and cushion of her own, and a window, permanently left open, leading out into the garden. Here she could live a life which, if lonely, was at least peaceful. And certainly until she grew too old to enjoy hunting at night I do not think she was unhappy. If the new territory was a small thing, it was at any rate her own.

Meanwhile Thai and Merlin had cemented their alliance and their acceptance of Wychwood with the catching of their first mouse in their new surroundings. Merlin flushed it somewhere out of cover and brought it, still alive and faintly kicking, into the house. Thai began to show interest, and Merlin promptly dropped the mouse which bolted for safety but was cornered against the doors of the garage, which happened to be closed. There, with a courage almost Spartan, it sat up on its hind legs, and when Merlin arrived promptly boxed his face. Merlin almost turned a cartwheel in his surprise. The mouse, I am happy to be able to record, managed to escape.

Merlin was a great player of games, especially with a ping-pong ball. He gradually evolved a game in which he 'defended' the goal of the sofa in our sitting-room, while my wife would try to bounce a ball over his head on to the cushions. He would spring up to catch really high throws with his paws, and could always be persuaded to play by the mere showing of a ping-pong ball.

He was also – in the summer – very responsive to the suggestion of an early morning walk, round about five o'clock, waltzing about the garden with a certain grave delight, which could be much in keeping with the mood of someone who had not slept too well. And he could learn from experience. He once leaped from my study-window on the house's first floor; looked extremely surprised on landing on his feet; and never repeated the performance.

Eleven

Which brings me automatically to the recording of an episode of which I can neither think nor write without that pricking of the eye-lids which accompanies both genuine grief and that easy sentimentality which comes almost as second nature to one who is to an extent conditioned by the theatrical temperament, and the – previously mentioned – Terry lachrymal glands.

Because primarily it was my fault. After what had befallen U-Puss I ought to have learned my lesson.

Like Omar's Bahram Merlin the Second was a 'great hunter'. And 'he liked to walk about at night'. As far as I am concerned it goes basically against the grain to interfere with a cat's individual idiosyncracies. I like to think of myself, if I ever do so in political terms, as a natural anarchist with mediaeval instincts! That a cat should wish to 'walk by himself' seems to me not only natural but essentially right. But the result of such indulgence may well in the outcome be tragic. And as it had been with U-Puss so it fell out with Merlin the Second. He went out one night on a hunting expedition, and early the next morning his body was found in the lane behind our house where he had been run over by a motor-car which – I need hardly add – had not bothered to stop.

I have on occasion been rebuked because, when driving a motor-car at night, I am inclined to choose the pace of the proverbial snail. The reason is quite simply that there is always in my imagination the picture of what I believe to have happened to Merlin. Too often have I seen the gleam of a cat's eyes as he starts to cross the road in the path of the car; to check and crouch as he is caught in the glare of the headlights. That is how I believe that Merlin met his fate, and – at the risk of being labelled as grotesquely soft-hearted – I would sooner drive permanently at some five miles per hour than cause anyone the sorrow which Merlin's death caused to my wife and myself.

We buried him next day, almost in the shade of the big chestnut-tree which, under the impulse of emergency, he had so often essayed to climb. Judy, who is as realist as she is warm-hearted and devoted to cats, insisted that the corpse should be shown to our other cats. She had a theory – and it proved well-founded – that to animals there is nothing terrible nor strange about Death. It is just a fact to be accepted. If Merlin just disappeared, so she maintained, his friends would miss him and would grieve accordingly. Seen dead he would be no more than something different and unacceptable. And to judge from results I think she was right. I confess that at the moment I found it heartless to watch Thai sniffing carelessly at that battered furry body.

I have to admit that for myself I have never been able to achieve conviction of the reality of a Future Life. I can only hope. But I have a curious instinct that for animals, who have been unable to plague the Almighty with their whinings and their self-excusings, there is almost certainly a Paradise. In that Paradise, well-watered and comfortably-cushioned, I feel sure that a place was prepared for Merlin. I feel also that Hugo, with U-Puss in rather diffident attendance, was there to make him welcome. He rests in the peace of the noble background of the Downs. And he is not forgotten. I like to think that his ghost may still walk in our little coppice, friendly, purring, and unafraid. . . .

Twelve

All of which may strike the reader as intolerably sentimental – a vice to which most writers about their pets are regrettably prone.

So it is time to exchange the Past for the Present; to consider the Cats that Are rather than the Cats that Have Been. To do so is a considerable consolation.

All the same I find it hard to put Merlin, as it were, 'into the discard', just as when I was a child I could not bear to throw away broken toys to which I had become attached. I remember a large and fubsy teddy-bear – but that is another story. . . .

In fact, even before Merlin's tragedy, we had decided – always remembering U-Puss – that we should make at least one more addition to our Feline Family, and that he should be a Burmese. For a time I hankered vaguely after an Abyssinian: a breed of which I knew nothing but had heard much, and that much fascinating. We found that not many miles away from us in Sussex there lived a lady who specialised in the breeding of the more exotic types: Siamese, Burmese, and Abyssinians. Accordingly we arranged to pay her a visit.

It was a remarkable experience. No cattery could have more obviously or definitely justified its description. Cats in stone, in china, and in plastic ornamented the little garden. Each room we entered crawled, literally, with kittens in and out of baskets, enjoying the most wonderful free-for-all time. A small boy, apparently the owner's son, seemed quite remarkably out of place, though also remarkably adapted to what must have been conditions of living of considerable discomfort. Behind the house a yard was lined with cages for breeding sires. They were vocal, but appeared quite happy.

On immediate show in the sitting-room were a very pregnant Abyssinian queen, and two litters of Burmese kittens, almost ready to leave home, from which we could make our choice. In addition, in the kitchen were a number of newly born Siamese, tended by an almost over-solicitous Siamese neuter. This last had been a show cat of considerable standing, until he had developed an eye infection which put him out of court from the point of view of showing or sale, but Mrs H. – as I shall call her – was not only a cat-breeder, but a cat-lover, and accordingly had not been able to persuade herself to let him be put down, and kept him accordingly as a sort of nurseman-in-chief.

With considerable difficulty we picked out a Burmese kitten, but in the event it turned out that the litter to which it belonged developed symptoms of a minor heart-ailment. Mrs H., being not only an admirable but a scrupulously honest character, refused to risk our being landed with a possible invalid, and so substituted for our original choice an alternative from a neighbouring cattery in Mayfield: a partially 'blue' Burmese kitten, who reached us in a state of considerable alarm – not surprising after a day or two spent in the mixed society of so many stranger cats – and promptly got on terms with Merlin by kissing him on the nose. (Thai incidentally was not amused.)

With U-Puss still in mind we christened the new arrival Nu-Puss. On arrival he looked like nothing so much as a small brown rat. It took some weeks before he developed sufficiently to prove his 'blue' attributes by displaying a curious blue sheen on his fur, particularly on the top of his head when he lay in the sunshine.

Our first association was hardly auspicious, as his first action, on being put in my study so as for the time being to be separated from the other cats, was to squeeze himself behind my bookshelves, where he stayed firmly for twenty-four hours, emerging only and very briefly to wolf a plate of chopped liver, to use his 'tray', and to swear in what was presumably some Eastern tongue whenever we did our best to lure him out. However, just when we were beginning to despair, and I was wondering whether I could get my shelves moved before he met the legendary fate of the unhappy bride who starved to death in the locked chest, he decided that we were reasonably acceptable, and that he would explore both house and garden.

He became, and remains to this day, a handful. He has also remained very much kitten rather than cat. Hence Nu-Puss as a name never really caught on, and he is known as KITTY-PUSS, to which he answers cheerfully enough. Merlin did all, and more, than could be expected in the capacity of peacemaker, but – and this I am sure is where recollection of U-Puss came in – Thai remained, and remains obdurate. It is almost as if Vietnam and Vietcong in miniature are represented under our roof. While U-Puss had been a big strong cat, Kitty-Puss is small, and by comparison weak in body if not in spirit. And I fancy that Thai, remembering the Burmese which had bullied him the past, now takes it out on the Burmese which, in his turn, he is big enough and strong enough to bully in the present. Whether it is because of colour or scent peculiar to Burmese I do not know. All I do know is that the feud persists, and shows no sign of dying. It is the more singular as Thai and Kitty-Puss sleep in the same kitchen – though each in his own basket – and have been known on occasion to eat out of the same plate. But for the most part their relationship varies from one of guarded neutrality to one of loudly and vigorously expressed hostility.

Thirteen

It would hardly be 'with it' in this day and age to ignore the effect, as I have seen it, made upon cats by television. My first set was installed in Long Acre by a paternal B.B.C. at the time I was so ill-advised as to accept supervision of Television Drama in addition to my radio responsibilities.

I was greatly interested to discover what the reactions of Merlin would be to the new and unfamiliar medium. It seemed that his first instinct was to treat it with contempt, as being without interest for him. Not even the *Wild Life* programmes which were, and in my opinion remain, among the very best of the Corporation's TV productions, stirred his curiosity. As far as he was concerned monkeys might chatter, birds might scream, even the larger cats might roar or growl – Merlin would merely blink wearily, curl up into a tighter ball than usual, and relax into peaceful slumber. I almost was compelled to the conclusion that a cat's vision did not include what appeared 'on the box'.

Yet there was one curious and startling exception. It only needed a game of association football to be televised for Merlin to spring into furious action. He would bound across the room, and run his paws up and down the tiny screen. If by chance he was sitting on top of the set – as occasionally he did, perhaps because of the warmth of its valves – he would lean over, and beat the screen's front with his paws. He made it very clear that the National Game held no charms for him.

I used to wonder if somewhere in his mind there might not lurk the hideous idea that all those heavy boots might be kicking about the field not a ball but a curled up cat.

In his turn, when the time came, Thai proved a supremely detached and unenthusiastic viewer. And neither our move to the country, nor the installation of a considerably improved and much larger set, did anything to change their attitude.

With this disinterest very much in mind I was the more curious to see the results when the time came for the cats themselves – Thai, Kitty-Puss and Minou – to face television cameras. I had compiled a Cat Anthology, and its publication had been thought worthy of inclusion as a news-item in a B.B.C. television programme. Accordingly a team of technicians, under the charming and professionally expert Miss Nancy Wise, descended upon Wychwood to put the cats and myself through our paces.

It must be admitted that the setting-up of the necessary gear – the cables, the microphones, the lights and the cameras – was regarded by the cats with a good deal of suspicion, so that I feared at the least a definite lack of cooperation, though I rather expected that Thai – whom I believe at heart to be something of an exhibitionist – would 'come good' when he found himself actually in the limelight. My idea for the basic set-up, with which Miss Wise was kind enough to agree, was that I should be interviewed with Thai posed beautifully on my lap, and with Kitty-Puss perhaps performing as an 'extra' in the background.

Thai had other ideas. He went cheerfully through all his tricks: rolling on the floor, stretching, crisping his claws, and so forth. But the paraphernalia of technology combined with the presence of a number of strangers proved too much for him. And nothing could persuade him not to glide swiftly and determinedly 'out of shot' at the moment critical for the camera-man. Kitty-Puss declined flatly to face the music, and retired into his private life in one of the upstairs rooms. It remained for Minou, like other veteran actresses, with whom on occasion I had been acquainted in a professional capacity, to 'steal the scene' with the most perfect certainty and aplomb. She posed herself with elegance. She faced the camera as if she had been making films all her days. She purred ecstatically, as if she had never been happier in her life. And she completed the performance by walking slowly and deliberately into a 'close-up' with an air that a Garbo or a Dietrich might well have envied. For one who, so my guilty conscience told me, tended to be 'despised and rejected' in comparison with her exotic companions, it was a remarkable achievement, and one for which I shall always be grateful. And I am glad that Minou should at least have 'had her hour'. She had earned it.

(I have been urged to insert at this point one practical hint for cat-lovers. Nowadays it is commonplace, and sensible common practice, to have cats injected at an early age against the more normal and deadly viruses, of which gastro-enteritis is perhaps the most virulent. But if the background is changed, as was the case when we forsook London for Sussex, it is advisable to repeat the injection process. It was owing to neglect of this precaution that we nearly lost Merlin shortly after the move. He dribbled incessantly; developed a badly ulcerated mouth; and smelled horrible – which was the more embarrassing as he only seemed comfortable when allowed to sleep in our bedroom. In the event a sympathetic and intelligent vet prescribed a course of a week's injections which did the trick. But it was a near thing.)

As a footnote to the television interview it may be worth recording that when it finally appeared 'on the box' we naturally brought in the cats to watch their reactions. They displayed imperturbable disinterest until the final close-up of Minou was backed by an unmistakeable purr – which, I am inclined to suspect, was probably 'dubbed' into the recording from some other source! At this point two pairs of ears were pricked up and twitched slightly. Nothing more. The hint might, I feel, be taken with profit by certain so-called television critics. . . .

Fourteen

While two of the most distinguished writers on the subject of Cats – Carl van Vechten, author of *The Tiger in the House*, and Rudyard Kipling who described 'the Wildest of all the Wild Animals was the Cat. He Walked by Himself, and all places were alike to him. . . .' – insisted on the basic and essential individualism and wildness of the Cat, it is my experience that while alone of the so-called domestic animals the cat follows sternly 'after his own thinking and his own desire' yet he adopts a pretty regular routine of his own existence, conditioned largely by the regularity with which he is offered his meals!

First of all, sleeping arrangements. Minou with her advancing years – she is now almost sixteen – spends most of her nights, and indeed her days, in her private boudoir where she can be certain of safety from molestation by Kitty-Puss or Thai. During the first two or three years of our occupation of Wychwood she spent almost all her time abroad, attending to her own affairs. I gathered that on occasion she would billet herself in the bedroom of one of our neighbours, who was handily adjacent, but not entirely susceptible to Minou's undoubted charm. Whether this night-walking of hers created for her a local reputation for availability or disreputability I cannot tell. As she was spayed as a kitten I think it unlikely. None the less in the seclusion appropriate to her age and dignity I find that my nose, apart from other indications of a slightly squalid kind, suggests that her permanently open window invites visitations from gentlemen-callers, and from time to time I have caught glimpses of a ginger tom with a white-ringed tail slinking along our boundary hedge with a distinctly furtive, if not conscience-stricken, air. But I do not care to cast unworthy aspersions upon a lady's reputation. In those early days she seemed to prefer to catch and enjoy her own food, leaving grisly remains of voles and field-mice in evidence outside our doorstep. Now it seems that hunting has lost its attraction for her, and she greets the arrival of her daily plate of food with ecstatic cries, and an endearing habit of standing up at full length on her hind legs, and scratching at the jamb of the door as high as she can reach.

Thai-Puss and Kitty-Puss sleep in the kitchen, each in his own basket, though in the winter Thai has been known to appropriate Kitty-Puss's basket because it is positioned nearer a radiator. While during the day they remain on permanently swearing rather than speaking terms, I can only recall two occasions when the feud has been given expression during hours of darkness. And then on descending irritably from the bedroom, having been roused by the racket, it was only to find that it amounted to no more than 'sound and fury, signifying nothing'.

When I go downstairs in the morning the first thing that I hear is the thump of Kitty-Puss jumping from his basket down on to the floor. As I go into the kitchen I find him stretching himself, apparently in two minds as to whether or not he would appreciate something in the way of breakfast. The conclusion of this debate is roughly fifty-fifty.

Thai on the other hand – and it must be made clear in his favour that he is now ten years old – reminds me in his behaviour of the more senior and respected members of my

London club. He is in no hurry to leave his basket. With a very occasional exception he displays no interest in breakfast. But, rather oddly, both he and Kitty-Puss stretch out welcoming necks for their respective collars, which are coloured respectively blue and green to match their owner's eyes, and carry metal labels with names and address – as a precaution in the event of straying – together with tiny bells.

The latter are carried in deference to the prejudices of our nearest neighbour, who is an addicted bird-fancier, and was in consequence more than a trifle disturbed when someone with a distorted sense of humour informed him that the new occupants of Wychwood intended bringing with them no fewer than seven cats!

Rather to my surprise the cats have never shown the least distaste for collars or bells, and I know few sounds more attractive than a faint tinkle from the depths of the shrubbery which betrays a feline approach. Also we are on the best of terms with our neighbour, a retired doctor of much personal charm, and need have no apprehension of his receiving any cat which he may observe in his garden with a pail of water or even a shot-gun!

The kitchen window is hardly opened before Kitty-Puss is through it, over the coal-bin beneath, and out into the garden for his early morning constitutional scurry. And for the expression of sheer physical beauty in action I know nothing to compare with that small brown bomb-shell of a cat springing in great leaps across the lawn towards the lime tree which he favours for claw-sharpening – or perhaps blunting. I can never decide which. The only parallel – and it is not as fanciful as it may sound – with this animal loveliness is the sight of a top-class polo pony coming through a hard game at full speed. And I have seen riders who spoil the perfection of that picture. . . .

As a rule Thai only leaves his basket about half an hour after Kitty-Puss's departure. It is his habit to pause on the kitchen window-sill, half in and half out of the window, while he appraises the quality of the day's weather. Standing so, snuffing the air, he reminds me of that character out of Dante's *Inferno*, who gave the impression that 'he held Hell in great contempt'. Thai, first thing in the morning, certainly gives me the feeling that he has doubts not only about our household and garden, but about the world and even the universe. Scepticism incarnate!

Having made up his mind – as a rule – that the temperature of the outside world is not much to his liking, Thai will also – as a rule – turn up his nose at any proffered breakfast, and make his way to the sitting-room where, like the clubmen aforesaid, he can find his favourite chair, or alternatively a patch of sunshine in which to lie. What seems to please him best – and again the club analogy holds – is to find and couch himself upon the one newspaper one wants at that moment to read. As the day wears on he may sit by the french window; may even take a dignified stroll as far as the vegetable-garden; may stretch himself out lazily on our little *patio*, for choice in the shade of a deck-chair; and will certainly use what must be the worst of Eastern tongues whenever Kitty-Puss appears round the corner of the house and engages attention.

Taken by and large Thai, possibly just because he is the elder of the two, is far more of a house-cat than Kitty-Puss, who tends to spend most of every day strictly minding his own business in some neighbouring field or garden. Usually he puts in a fleeting appearance shortly after midday, but while Thai is invariably on hand at lunch-time, gazing upwards with the wide blue eyes of almost pathetic innocence for tit-bits – which I am ashamed to say are nearly always forth-coming – Kitty-Puss seems neither to expect nor to relish such off-the-cuff snacks.

Between half-past four and five in the afternoon both cats make it abundantly clear that the vital moment of their day is at hand. Thai makes no bones about it, and is proportionately clamorous. But generally speaking it is not long before Kitty-Puss emerges from the coppice, a rhododendron bush, or the field of sweet-corn behind the house, to establish his claim to his share of the main meal of the day.

In our experience, for what it may be worth, we have found that they need, appreciate, and are gratifyingly healthy on a diet of between two and three ounces of raw meat each day, apart from the occasional breakfast out of tin or packet.

This meat, which I imagine to be horse-meat for the most part, is procured from a local slaughter-house in Ringmer – an expedition which I admit to finding rather revolting, though the butchers are invariably helpful, and appear fundamentally humane – and then must be chopped into comparatively small pieces before serving: a process as necessary as it is unpleasant.

The cutting-up is always accompanied by what may reasonably be described as an *oratorio* for two voices, with Thai very much in the lead, though Kitty-Puss makes a by no means contemptible contribution. The ensuing silence, insufficiently prolonged, is astonishing, and both cats like an after-dinner bout of exercise, presumably to assist digestion.

Minou simply bolts her food, and re-settles herself to the sleep which for her has now become almost second nature.

After which reference to intake it seems only natural – and even right in this Permissive Day and Age – to make, with all appropriate delicacy, some mention of 'output'.

It is of course well known that, certainly in comparison with dogs, cats are by nature both fastidious and cleanly in their habits. Mother-cats may often be observed instilling such habits into their kittens. In my experience both Siamese and Burmese are notable for the importance they give to personal hygiene. In the case of Kitty-Puss delicacy is pushed to a length almost obsessive: he is most disinclined to perform his natural functions in the presence of others – not only of humans, but even of Thai.

The latter is also an admirably clean cat, unless something he has eaten has disagreed with him, when he tends apparently to spend many of the hours of darkness propelling himself around the kitchen floor on his behind. The consequences, particularly when contemplated first thing in the morning, are not agreeable. What is worse is the fact that while he is passionately devoted to fish he also devours it so greedily and rapidly that he is quite unable to digest it, and returns it almost as quickly as it has been swallowed!

I was brought up in the tradition which forbade the mentioning of a lady's name 'in the mess', particularly if such mention might reflect upon her reputation. It is therefore with cheeks faintly reddened that I have to admit that with advancing years Minou, like other elderly ladies, has grown increasingly incontinent. She has of course her own tray in her private 'boudoir', sited beneath the shelf which was specially made for her, and on which she spends so much of her time. Unfortunately her use of it is spasmodic rather than regular, as the result presumably of having had at her disposal the whole of the outside world. With increasing age this Great Outside would seem to have lost much of its appeal, and in consequence the atmosphere of the 'boudoir' is on occasion less savoury than one could wish. . . .

For Thai and Kitty-Puss during the summer months there is no problem. There are flower-beds. There is a shrubbery – not to mention our immediate neighbour's flower-beds and shrubbery. There is even a tiny coppice. But as the nights draw in, the temperature falls, and the tops of warm radiators increase their appeal, a tray becomes a necessity during the night-season, and its cleaning the first of the early morning chores.

I would only add that it is as vital to give cats the opportunity to keep themselves clean as it is to keep them regularly and healthily fed. Cats go by instinct a very long way towards looking after themselves. But once established in a household they demand attention as well as affection. Deprived of either they will not be happy. And I would be inclined to claim that of all unhappy animals an unhappy cat is the unhappiest – and the most capable of making that unhappiness only too evident. Stroking and patting, rubbing beneath the chin, the odd saucer of cream, will all be appreciated. They are not enough. What is enough can only be learned by consistent study of your own cat. And like most other things that are worth while, it has to be worked for. In brief, a cat should always be thought of as an individual, not as a toy.

Part II

Sternly Impersonal

So the cats whom one has loved, and, alas, for the most part lost, dissolve into the mists of memories. It is a curious picture, singularly disjointed, rather as if a film was being run through on an out-of-date projector. To a large extent it consists of a sequence of 'close-ups': of glowing eyes, of glossy fur, of tails held proudly erect or curled quietly across noses; of Hugo's dark head beside mine on the pillow; of Merlin the First singing in his tree; of U-Puss so carelessly supercilious among the dogs at Cowdray; of Bronx asleep in the sunshine; of Merlin the Second amiably purring; of Thai-Puss unamiably swearing; of Minou so somnolent and static; of Kitty-Puss racing at speed across a lawn as though his objective was the sky-line of the Downs across the Ouse valley; of that Siamese cat seen so long ago in Gledhow Gardens trotting at his red-haired mistress's heels. . . .

In my mind the pictures jerk into perspective; fade to be replaced by others; ultimately dissolve into the blankness of that dark screen from which there is no return.

But if the recording of memories is desirable or worth while, why choose the memories of cats? Can such a choice be justified? Do they really rate as so important among the threads which have composed the tapestry of a life for the most part unimportant, and yet in its own way reasonably and sufficiently variegated?

There have been the people one has known – many of them

interesting beyond the ordinary. There have been the places one has visited, and when such include Delphi, Athens, Taormina, New York, San Francisco and Oklahoma surely one cannot have travelled altogether in vain. There has been one's working life which, while in the long run was probably without significance, having regard to the essentially transitory quality of all radio, none the less – I dare to assert – made a certain impact upon drama in general during the thirties and forties.

So why choose cats as the subject of record?

I might retort flatly, in the terms of the 'permissive society', that I wanted to write this book, and that in that wanting can be found adequate justification. I might try to pile the Pelion of explanation upon the Ossa of excuse.

I prefer to quote from Walt Whitman – and I do not think I could do better:

> I think I could turn and live with animals.
> They are so placid and self-contained.
> I stand and look at them, and long, and long.
> They do not sweat and whine about their condition,
> They do not lie awake in the dark and weep for their sins,
> They do not make me sick, discussing their duty to God;
> Not one is dissatisfied, not one is demented with the mania of owning things;
> Not one kneels to another, nor to his kind that lived thousands of years ago.
> Not one is respectable and unhappy over the whole earth.

I fear I cannot go as far as Carl van Vechten, who wrote about cats with such affection and comprehension, in his attempt to show that the Cat is of all mammals the highest expression of civilised living. I should like to be able to agree. I regret that, taken by and large, Self-Sufficiency is not in all respects satisfactory as a philosophy or a guide to behaviour.

But it seems to me that in their different ways Whitman and van Vechten had the root of the matter in them. They faced, and were appalled by, the short-comings of Natural Man, who has made such an unholy mess of all his advantages. They saw in the Cat a creature who is always, no matter what his breeding or conditions of existence, the Master of his Fate, and no matter how bloody remains unbowed.

'We may dominate dogs,' wrote van Vechten, 'but cats can never be dominated except by force. They can be annihilated; at least a few of them can, but never made servile or banal. The cat is never vulgar.' (This, I feel, is his greatest title to fame.) He will not permit even God to interfere with his liberty, and if he suffers as much as a toothache he will refuse all food. He would rather die than endure pain. Thus, like the Spartan, he preserves the strength of his stock. . . . There is indeed no single quality of the cat that man could not emulate to his advantage. He is clean; the cleanest indeed of all animals. . . . He is silent, walking on padded paws with claws withdrawn, making no sound unless he wishes to say something definite. . . . Nothing will make a cat stop talking when he wants to, except the hand of death. He is entirely self-reliant. He lives in homes because he chooses to do so, and as long as the surroundings and the people suit him; but he lives there on his own terms, and never sacrifices his own comfort or his own well-being for the sake of the stupid folk with whom he comes in contact. Thus he is the most satisfactory of friends. . . . He is modest. He is urbane. He is dignified. . . . The cat makes no boast of his pre-eminent position. He is content to occupy it. . . .'

With the greater part of all this I find myself, in the light of my own experience with cats, almost entirely in agreement. The single doubt remains. Can such an apotheosis of selfishness be justified in the long run? Is there not a flaw in the spur, a worm in the bud?

'Cats', retorts van Vechten, 'seldom interfere with other people's rights. . . . They never write operas. . . . They never sign papers nor pay taxes, or vote. . . . An injunction will have no power whatever over a cat. . . . He would refuse to obey the Constitution itself.'

All of which sounds very well. The trouble is that human beings are not cats. They cannot wear the armour of absolute self-containment. Worst of all, men and women are sentimental, and, deprived of this sentimentality, they tend to feel deprived simultaneously of their humanity. The average human will undoubtedly claim and assert that cats are heartless. He might conceivably ask himself the question as to whether the English novelist did not have something when he ended a chapter with the reflection 'No use to have a heart!' And he did not belong to the contemporary or 'trendy' brigade. He was in fact that most old-fashioned of types John Galsworthy.

And maybe there are worse things than writing operas – even than paying taxes. And where would poor Mankind be without its multitude of Constitutions?

Is the Cat then to be considered basically and simply as wild animal, which has acquired a certain aura of domestic respectability, merely because various of the trappings of domesticity – warmth, regular meals, affection displayed within reason – happen to suit him? In brief, can the Cat really be tamed? Here it seems to me that the evidence is conflicting.

I have seen several Siamese, apart from Nara's, who have apparently adapted themselves without resentment to collar and lead. Hugo would put up with nothing of the kind. U-Puss accepted his with a certain resignation, but clearly without enthusiasm. Minou, before she grew too old any longer to enjoy exercise, would accompany us on quite long walks. She would even 'sit' on command and wait patiently for our return. (On one such occasion she was forgotten until after darkness had fallen, and was found sitting patiently on the precise spot where she had been left.) Merlin the Second was always more than ready for a game of his own invention with a ping-pong ball. But the game was essentially his, not ours. I fancy that the Call of the Wild is always faintly audible in the Cat's inner ear; that in the long run he will respond to it.

There is of course the long-haired, usually Persian, variety to which personally I have never been drawn, and which always reminds me of the character who 'sat on a cushion, sewed a fine seam, and fed upon strawberries sugar and cream'. Such cats are certainly decorative, may well be affectionate, and are an ornament to any establishment. For me they are not cats. They might almost as well be stuffed – and there an end. But it is neither fair nor kind to pass comment upon a breed of which I have no personal experience, and the Persian Cat has after all a long-established tradition behind him to support his claim both to Dignity and Impudence. I have little doubt that he can look after himself. . . .

What is surely unarguable is the fact that the Cat represents the ultimate of physical beauty as expressed in flesh and blood. I would not go so far as seriously to compare the lithe elegance of a cat on a wall, or in the crotch of a tree with the Parthenon, the cliff-face of Delphi, San Francisco's Golden Gate, or the Grand Canyon. But with the possible exceptions of the cheetah, the Bengal tiger, and the black leopard – all of them after all simply outsize cats – I have seen no animal which can stand comparison with the Cat. To consider mankind in this connection would be laughable, if it were not pathetic. The 'two-forked radish' is seldom even a pretty sight, especially when stripped to the buff. He is clumsy. He is physically weak. His features are too often squashed out of regularity. Even athletes are seldom truly graceful. To prove the case I would only invite the reader to view, without prejudice in favour of his own kind, people in buses or tube trains or crowds. We are, and we must face it, a plain and dingy lot, and the Technological Age, designed to enable us to live with the minimum of trouble and physical exertion, has done nothing to improve any beauty that we might have.

Just as the Cat refuses to be tamed, so he cannot be civilised, and it would seem that he is all the better as a result. He has not got the traditional reputation for having nine lives without justification. He earns every one of those nine by his independence, his perfect eye for the main chance, his admirable sense of priorities, his agility, his balance, his freedom from any sort of humbug.

He has also infinite patience – a virtue of which most politicians could take note with advantage!

But what of the Cat's future in what seems likely to be known as the Age of Pollution: an age when motor-ways and synthetic building projects are being continually expanded at the expense of the countryside; the trees, the hedges and the Wet Wild Woods?

Of the Cat's ultimate survival I have little or no doubt. Should our planet one day – following upon that Atomic Bomb explosion which has so bemused and befuddled so many of the contemporary generation – be visited by curious space-travellers from the Moon or Mars I believe that it is more than likely that their first Earthly experience will be the sight of a cat, completely occupied with the business of washing himself on some open space chosen with his usual sagacity as being free alike of rubble and contamination. Being free of the fears induced by the over-sensitive imaginations of human beings his nervous system will have remained unaffected and in good shape. If man has destroyed himself it is certain that rats will remain, and as long as there are rats no cat is likely to stay hungry for long. It is hardly a cheerful picture to imagine: cats chasing rats across the desert of an empty world. But in fact is it any less tolerable than those landscapes of Verdun and the First Day of the Somme Battle in 1916? I wonder, but I am inclined to doubt it.

It must always be remembered that the Cat was once a god – in ancient Egypt. I believe I am right in saying that he does not appear in Homer – here the dog-lover has the edge with the touching tale of Odysseus' dog who dies on his master's return – and that he is first mentioned in European literature by Herodotus: *ailouros*, the tail-waver, an animal first met with by the Greeks in Egypt, and thereafter exported from that granary of the Empire both to Greece and Italy. There is mention in archaeological records of a scene on an Athenian vase: of a boy on his way to school with his accompanying slave holding a cat on a leash. And Italian vases of the classical era show women playing with perfectly recognisable cats.

But cats were rare in Europe before Christianity attacked the hierarchy of the old pagan gods – and with the advent of Christianity came their identification with the Evil One himself. From which emerged the tradition that only the wrong type of person likes cats, just as in most English short stories the right sort of person always loves dogs.

Not that all cats are amiable any more than all dogs are detestable and unclean. Cats may be intelligent, attractive to watch, hygienically unexceptionable. To achieve their owner's affection they must also have the indefinable quality of charm. Hugo possessed it. U-Puss and Kitty-Puss respectively had and have it. Thai lacks it. I feel this is rather unfair. It is also unfortunately true. But it is an unfair world in which we live. How does Providence justify one woman being born with a hare-lip and a squint, while another becomes Miss World of 1972 with no apparent qualifications other than certain physical statistics? It is just too bad – but maybe compensations exist in another and better world. One would like to think so. . . .

The relationship of cats with children is a curious one. Most young children tend to love them simply as soft warm furry toys to be played with. Kipling, who knew most things, tells us that the Cat 'will play with the Baby as long as he does not pull his tail too hard'. Contrariwise I have found that my own cats have no doubt on the subject. They frankly detest children. They find them noisy, clumsy, and potentially frightening. It only needs the patter of tiny feet on the stairs, and the cry of childish voices in the lobby for Thai and Kitty-Puss simultaneously to bolt for cover, usually under a bed in the spare room.

At the risk of being classed with Herod I am inclined to believe that it is largely the children's fault. They clutch. They grab. They scream. Nowadays too few of them have been taught 'to be seen and not heard'. It seems to me that they offend my cats' dignity, and the latter is as precious to him as his food and his warm basket.

I have read that cats are both colour-blind and tone-deaf. It may be true. But as for the latter it has been pointed out with justice that if the Cat needs music he is more than capable of providing his own. As for the latter he is not – and he may thank God for the fact – concerned with changing traffic-lights!

On the other hand I know from experience that a cat, faced by his own reflection in a mirror, will almost always display profound disinterest, while the presence of another cat, while invisible to me, is immediately apparent to him. Which gives me the idea that his nose is more important to him than his eyes; indeed that it is the most vital of his senses.

As I have written earlier I did not intend in this book to get drawn into the conventional, and to me rather tedious cat-versus-dog controversy. It is a subject that has been done to death, and might now surely be left to moulder quietly in the grave! However, someone who has cast an eye, for the most part approving, over this script has told me flatly that to dodge this issue implies lack of courage or lack of conviction – probably both. So the gauntlet, having been flung down, must be picked up. Naturally I declare my interest. I prefer cats to dogs. I have kept a number of cats. I have only once given house-room to a dog, and that unwillingly. So I must do what I can to avoid seeming to cog the dice.

On the whole I am inclined to feel that the ferocity of the traditional feud tends to be a good deal exaggerated.

If kittens and puppies are brought up together cheek by jowl from their earliest days it is seldom that no permanent *modus vivendi* is established. I have frequently been told touching stories of bitches who have adopted motherless kittens, and of large dogs which have adopted the role of elderly and protective uncle in similar cases. I have no reason to doubt the accuracy of such tales, though dog-lovers may seem to paint such pictures in oppressively primary colours.

My own, purely personal, view is that the original conflict stems from one simple physical fact: the cat can always climb a tree; the dog cannot. The resentment of the dog in consequence is altogether comprehensible. To understand it it is only necessary to watch for a few minutes a dog standing on his hind legs, scratching impotently at a tree-trunk with blunted claws, while a cat sits calmly in the branches above his head, with knowledge of his own security combined with a certain contempt in every line of his attitude.

The clash between cat-lovers and dog-lovers is in all respects more deep-seated. It is clouded invariably both by prejudice and by sentiment – neither the most reliable of counsellors. Of course, if you are a hearty uncomplicated extrovert the dog must be your choice. His reactions are simple. His loyalty is obvious. His affections are demonstrative. His practical uses – as gun-dog, as watch-dog, as racing-dog – are considerable. Many dogs are beautiful – though by no means all. I recall with the extreme of pleasure the sight of red setters standing in the sunshine – and, by contrast, the loathesome aspect of those over-fed, over-indulged, and permanently snuffling pug-dogs, which seemed in my youth one of the invariable accompaniments to the presence of elderly and over-dressed ladies.

The other basic difference between the species, by no means to be bridged, is that while the dog is only happy in attached servility, and will even lick the hand that beats him, the cat is only happy in freedom. Without granting him equivalent respect you cannot hope to keep a cat. He will see you damned and himself starving first. It would be fascinating to know how the Egyptians succeeded in turning their cat-god into a domestic animal. However, the trappings of worship can become tedious, and it may be that the priests of Bubastis concerned themselves more with ritual than with diet. Which may have done the trick.

The dog is inclined to hysteria. Shut him out – for no matter what perfectly good reason – and he howls, scratches, raises all the hell he can. Shut out a cat, and in nine cases out of ten, after a glance back of combined pity and incomprehension, he will stroll away intent on alternative distraction, probably to discover and make use of some different entrance to your dwelling of which you have never suspected the existence. I believe it was Mahomet, a gentleman not without influence even to this day, who said that 'he loved the cat for his refinement, and despised the dog for his want of any'.

For the introvert, on the other hand, there can only be one possible choice: the cat. Between them there is an instinctive sympathy. The introvert longs, though he seldom succeeds in his desire, to be self-sufficient. The cat *is* self-sufficient, almost without trying. The introvert, while frequently humane almost to a fault, is fundamentally selfish. The same is true of the cat, and I do not believe that he would seek either to apologise for or nor to justify his attitude. A Mr Oswald Crawfurd has written in *Round the Calendar*: 'Rather than consort with a bully, a villain, a ruffian or a sneak, the cat will part company with his owner; and scrupulously clean himself, the cat loves those only who are as scrupulous as himself in this respect. Rather than live with persons who fail to come up to his standards, morally or physically, he will abandon the house and take to the woods. Therefore a man's companionship with cats is as good as a certificate of character to him. It takes perception keener than is common to interpret the language of the cat, the often silent language of his looks and attitudes. The dog, on the other hand, is demonstrative; any casual person can guess what he means; but he is far too often over-demonstrative, and his heart often gets the credit for what is often nothing but foolish sentimental gush. The dog is greedy and sudden in wrath, and can place no restraint upon his anger and his voracity. The cat on the other hand is a model of abstemiousness and can keep his temper. . . .'

The lily may have been gilded. Its essence remains true for all that. While admitting my prejudice I feel entitled to call my witnesses. After all, man is only an animal too.

In the other camp stands the authority who described the Cat as 'probably the least useful of domestic animals'. From the entirely human standpoint this is true enough. The Cat does not provide milk, steaks or cutlets. He is hardly adequate as guardian of the house. He produces nothing in the shape of material wealth, just as he neither writes operas nor pays taxes. But in respect of personal loyalty – and this is what has always damned the Cat in the eyes of the average respectable and middle-class Englishman – there is not and cannot be comparison between Dog and Cat. For the former it is *sine qua non*. For the latter it appears neither sensible nor comprehensible. The value to civilised man of personal loyalty is immeasurable. It must have covered as great a multitude of stupidities as it has sins. It is one of the virtues that has enabled Man to claim superiority over the Beasts, and in consequence places the Cat finally and for ever among the latter. And I doubt if any of the most ardent of the pro-Cat faction have yet been found to adopt the logical conclusion that the greatest patriots from Leonidas to Churchill proved little more by their actions than that they were a particularly superior brand of Dog! If it is objected that Patriotism and Personal Loyalty are not the same thing, I would suggest that the first is only an extension of the second, with the loyalty applied to Country as opposed to Individual. And for the Cat the world is his oyster; for the Dog his Master is the world. The two points of view are incompatible, and must be accepted as such.

I regret it. I would find the world a poorer place without dogs, as I would find it – once having known them as companions – intolerable without cats. The choice in fact has to be made. And just as the introvert, the writer or the artist, has to put up with the philistine extrovert, *le moyen homme sensuel*, so the extrovert must endure with such philosophy as he can muster the introvert's preference for the Cat with his independence, his beauty, and his self-sufficiency, as opposed to the Dog with his loud mouth, his far from cleanly habits, the frequently slavering expression of his affection.

It is only fair to repeat that only once in my life have I shared a dwelling with a dog – and the dog was not mine. It never bit me. It accepted its food with apparent gratitude and pleasure. It was not unreasonably noisy. And such pleasure as I might have gained from its society was largely vitiated by my having to take it out for a walk last thing at night through the by-ways of Long Acre, until it could make up its mind regarding the selection of a lamp-post. This proceeding I found cold, boring, and uncomfortable. I found inadequate consolation in finding my hand surreptitiously licked, or in watching a tail unexpectedly wagged. In short we were not *sympathique*. That was all there was to it. And having known to my cost for years that I was helplessly and hopelessly introvert, I should have known better than to try the experiment. The fault was mine, not the dog's.

There have been times in the country when the picture has appealed to me, in imagination, of my walking the fields with a dog, preferably one of the larger breeds, trotting obediently at my heels. I should be carrying a heavy stick, and there would be a straight-grained pipe between my teeth. I should stride along with the wind in my hair and the sunshine on my face, like the girl in the song who was 'told by Mother and Father she was rather Bold and Free'. The reality returns to wipe out the picture. Thai would actively rebel. Kitty-Puss would almost certainly seek a Better 'Ole and go to it. The thing simply would not work, and it is as well to realise as much.

In the Bible, as in Homer, the Cat would seem to have been monstrously – I almost wrote 'disgracefully' – neglected. In the Old Testament he does not appear at all, though I have seen it suggested that in two passages from Isaiah the word 'satyrs' probably refers in fact to cats. But the evidence strikes me as thin.

Again, in the New Testament there are only three references to connect the Cat with the Life of Our Lord, and they appear not in the Gospels nor the Epistles but in an apocryphal work called *The Gospel of the Holy Twelve*. These are in the tradition of the better-known parables, and the most charming perhaps is one in which a mother-cat with kittens plays a part analogous to that of The Woman Taken in Adultery, and a crew of heartless villagers are rebuked by Jesus accordingly.

Also I have seen in a picture – I am almost certain it was in Venice – a cat included among the animals surrounding the manger of the Nativity. But for genuine cat-addiction among ecclesiastics we have to wait for the French Cardinal Richelieu, who is almost invariably presented in the company of one or more white cats. Worthy also of remembrance is that man of acknowledged sanctity, St Philip Neri, who, when absent from his home, was in the habit of sending urgent letters of enquiry regarding the health of his cats; and that Prince of South Wales, Hywel Dda, who in the year 936 A.D. enacted a law for the Protection of Cats: one of the first of legal records. Clearly he knew his business, and with all due respect I would urge a study of him upon today's Prince Charles.

I must return briefly, and albeit unwillingly, to the subject of Cruelty – not only to cats, but to animals in general. I thing we owe a debt to Miss Olivia Manning for reminding us that Sadism may often begin with animals. It seldom stops there. It may be that in some sort this reaction is provoked by the Cat's inherent and unwavering independence; his determination to remain in essence a wild rather than a domestic animal. Kipling's Man would always throw anything available at the Cat. Kipling's Dog would always chase the Cat up the nearest tree. The Cat might be *in* the Cave. He was not *of* it. It was his lot to suffer accordingly.

However, let us be in the fashion, and fall back for support upon statistics. In 1966 the British Veterinary Association stated that four million animal experiments are carried out yearly, 'just over 12,000 being surgical operations on unanaesthetised cats, dogs and horses'. It is enough to turn the stomach, not only of an unabashed cat-lover, but of any reasonable humane and civilised individual. How much in the way of greed, vanity, unthinking stupidity, and heartbreak of pets' owners is represented by figures such as these? We no longer bait bulls or bears. We condemn the bloody brutality of the Spanish bull-fight, *pace* the late Mr Hemingway. We should be ashamed to do otherwise. Yet we cheerfully hand over the cat and dog to the tender mercies of self-styled scientists who almost certainly, like the judges in the Dreyfus Case, 'sleep well at night and have wives and children whom they love'.

One would like to think that these horrors arise from nothing worse – if there is anything worse – than mere lack of imagination. It is a comforting theory, but it will not stand up to the facts. Vivisection of animals is still being justified on pseudo-scientific grounds, though when recently it was averred that certain elderly and almost certainly mortally ill human beings were being experimented upon from a similar angle, a cry of horror and revolt was splashed across most of the newspapers in the land. In this country most of us are supposed to live according to a creed whose basis depends upon the saying 'Do unto Others as you would they should do unto you.' Yet I doubt if much support would be found for the suggestion that a naked man, in full possession of his senses, should be flung into a cage with a hungry tiger to prove that the latter is more ferocious and could spring faster than the former. One cannot help wondering from time to time how the vivisectionist would fancy a taste of his own medicine. One would almost – I repeat almost – like to see!

In ancient Egypt it was a capital crime to kill a cat. Life imprisonment, now that capital punishment has been abolished by collective humane opinion, might be just about adequate for the torturers of helpless and unanaesthetised animals. Though, personally, I would prefer them to be confined in a specially constructed laboratory, in which they could practise on each other to their hearts' content in the intervals of listening to carefully selected passages from H. G. Wells' *Island of Doctor Moreau*. I do not feel that it is an exaggeration to suggest that any person who torments animals – no matter how apparently lofty his motive – is a potential murderer. And while we no longer hang murderers we have not as yet reached the stage of considering their activities worthy of emulation or stimulation.

No doubt some reader will be found seeking to controvert me by the flat question 'So I suppose you are a vegetarian?' I am not, and so must plead guilty to living on the flesh of some of the animals concerning whom I seem to feel so extravagantly. Nor am I quite sure that it is adequate defence for me to retort that I find it as natural to eat a steak as it is natural for a cat to devour a sparrow. What I can say definitely is that if I thought, even more if I knew, that butchers' raw material came from beasts that were tortured before being killed, I would turn vegetarian tomorrow. Which is why I view with ever-increasing distaste such commercial progressiveness as the keeping of battery hens, and the breeding of calves that never see the light of day. We must eat to live, and despite the great age attained by Bernard Shaw I am not convinced that the synthetic nut-cutlet is as nourishing as the mutton-chop. It is certainly less appetising. And I do not think I am maligning the memory of a dead man in repeating the story that in his later years G.B.S. was considerably stimulated by doses of extract of liver!

The least we can do for the animals which we sacrifice to our needs and appetites is to ensure that they are provided with all possible amenities – fresh air, green grass being the most important – while they are alive; and that we make certain both that they are not terrified before their deaths; and that those deaths should be quick, certain, and uncomplicated. Once again, no more than the minimum of imagination is required, so that no *abattoir* can be equated with a mediaeval torture-chamber. There is no one of us who can escape a degree of personal responsibility in this matter. We should not seek to dodge it.

It is curious, even a little disgusting, that regard for animals should not have kept pace with the apparent increasing acceptance of the value of the individual human life. Never has that value been so publicised, nor more fantastically exaggerated. For fear of Death, which is after all as inevitable an ingredient in the business of living as Birth, mankind has cowered for two decades under the shadow of the atomic bomb, though the simple Italian peasant continues to cultivate his tiny vineyard on the slopes of Etna or Vesuvius, imperturbable in the face of what he has learned to regard as incomprehensible if merciless Acts of God. Western Civilisation prides itself on its abolition of torture and the rope as a symptom of its realisation of 'man's inhumanity to man'. We have grown very solicitous for the safety of our own skins. Quite a number of people are actively distressed when they hear of children dying by the thousand of hunger or disease, even if their skins be brown or yellow. Must our imagination, and in consequence our mercy, stop short of practical sympathy with the dog and the cat? If so, it is to our lasting shame. And we had better do something about it.

I remember a play written many years ago for radio by the late Lord Dunsany, in which Man was arraigned before a jury of the Animals. Man sought in vain for an advocate, until at last one was found to address the Court on his behalf. The defender proved to be the Mosquito. For him alone Man had been both a benefactor and a necessity. It is hardly necessary to labour the moral of what proved a most engaging and effective flight of imagination.

I may seem to have strayed considerably from the main theme of this book: a description of the cats who have shared and contributed so richly to my life over the years. But what I have just written – though there is nothing original about it – calls for repetition, lest like other obvious truths it is forgotten or disregarded.

However, it is probably time to return for a final glance at Minou, dreaming away the hours of her declining years in the seclusion of her 'boudoir'; at Thai-Puss stretched out in a patch of sunshine with his coat gleaming and his claws crisping; at Kitty-Puss, alternately sprawled on top of a radiator – there is no doubt of cats' general approval of central heating – or chasing leaves along our little terrace with that kittenish abandon which he has never lost.

By way of that faulty projector, for so I feel inclined again to define my memory, the pictures from the past take blurred shape, fall into focus, merge one into the other, and so fade: that first Siamese of Nara's in Gledhow Gardens so long ago; Bronx asleep on his wall in Kensington Place; Lulu and her uncounted lovers; Hugo's chocolate mask beside me on the pillow; Merlin the First climbing, and scarring, my book-backs; Hugo regarding the Second German War in general, and Evesham in particular with a certain withdrawn contempt; Merlin the Second, whom of all the cats I have known I would choose to call without qualification essentially *good*; U-Puss driving assorted dogs into hysterics at Cowdray Park. . . .

The screen goes blank, and, altogether absurdly, I find my eyes filling with tears. And not for the first time I ask myself why it is next thing to impossible to write about animals without indulging in sentimentality, occasionally mawkish. Such a minor classic of the *genre* as *Jock of the Bushveld* is nearly spoiled by it. Not all the stories from the deservedly famous *Jungle Books* – in particular *The White Seal* – can entirely escape the charge. Is the answer merely that human beings have only two attitudes to adopt towards animals: one of indifference, which only too often includes cruelty; or one of over-absorption which, perhaps as a makeweight to the aforesaid indifference, can too easily slop over into that sentimentality which is a favourite form of self-indulgence? That the Cat neither understands nor sympathises with this particular attitude may well account for his never having been able to achieve the domestic status of the Dog, of the family status of the Horse. Speak of the Dog, and the hearer thinks of the Sportsman. Speak of the Horse, and the hearer thinks of the Gentleman, raised by his mount above the common herd. Speak of the Cat, and the hearer thinks automatically of the Outlaw, who makes his own laws, and cheerfully feels justified in breaking any others.

Not that this feline characteristic has saved writers from falling into the trap. I would not be so unkind as to quote examples, confining myself to the sardonic reflection that I am myself one of the guilty. Is it perhaps that the Cat, while addicted to conversation, remains dumb and unable to speak for himself? Or is there some inherently sentimental ingredient in soft fur, and large unwinking eyes? It well may be so.

EPILOGUE

The picture is, to the best of my poor ability, completed. Certainly Thai-Puss agrees with me. He has just sidled round the door into my study, making no bones about the fact that I seem to need to be reminded of his dinner-hour, and that the clatter of plates is infinitely to be preferred to the clatter of a typewriter. Below me through my window I can see Kitty-Puss racing madly about the garden with that 'wind in his tail' which makes one of the glories of an autumn day. Minou, I know, is peacefully asleep, and happily free of any inclination to be disturbed.

To those, my three cats, it may seem ungrateful that I should have to admit that I write these final paragraphs under the influence of a certain melancholy. (Like the wind this may be no more than one of the normal accompaniments of the autumn season of the year.)

As one grows older one comes to accept the fact of Death as inevitable, and the loss of beloved friends as perhaps the most disagreeable aspect of the business of living, which must nevertheless be accepted with such philosophy as one can muster. In a queer way I have never been able to accept the loss of a cat with any degree of complaisance. This may sound both exaggerated and unfeeling. It is true for all that. Perhaps it arises from the fact that only too often a cat's death has been violent or unnecessary or both. And automatically I resent the needless and the violent. One accepts the stark reality which limits the cat's life-span compared with a man's. One revolts against idle circumstances which shatter that life-span. It is like the breaking of a mirror: the destruction of something irreparable; of something designed for beauty, and almost deserving of immortality.

Is one straining too hard at drawing the bow? And is the bow no more than the proverbial 'long-bow' of emotional exaggeration? If so, like others, I must abide the issue. I have not attempted a Treatise on the subject of the Nature of the Feline Tribe. I have had no earth-shattering discoveries to recount about cats. I have tried, as simply as may be, to tell of the cats I have known, of what I have gained from their companionship, and of their effect upon my life.

At that – blowing my nose with some severity, and assuring Thai that his meal will not be long delayed – I must leave it.

I feel that the account would be fairer, better – certainly better-balanced – if I had been able to include in it what Bronx or Hugo thought, what Thai and Kitty-Puss think, about *me*. That would really be illuminating. But just as 'cats do not write operas' so also they do not write books. And for the sake of man's peace of mind perhaps it is just as well!

Afterword

To round out this record it is necessary, if melancholy, to be compelled to add as a footnote that since the above was written we have lost Minou.

She had attained the ripe age of fifteen years, and towards the end of 1971 was beginning to show signs of it. She no longer walked nor hunted by night to lay voles or field-mice on our doorstep. She tended to a philosophic immobility. But her appetite remained good, and except for occasional bouts of distressing incontinence on the whole she seemed well enough.

At the beginning of this year my wife and I left England for a three months' cruise. Wychwood we left in the care of our friends the Paskins from Barcombe village, who on a previous occasion had done us a similar service, looking after the house, and proving devoted to the cats.

All seemed well on our return at the end of March, but we noticed that Minou seemed less inclined than ever to go out and take exercise. She drowsed and slept, and drowsed again. We grew anxious about her, and decided at Easter that as soon as the holidays were over we would have her overhauled thoroughly by our excellent vet, and get his opinion of her expectation of life.

Minou was to spare him the trouble, and us the heart-ache of decision about her future. On Easter Monday she must have had some sort of stroke. She could only wander aimlessly in a circle, and had almost lost the use of her back legs. We took her out to lie on her cushion in the sunshine. And it was in that sunshine and with as I hope the rising scents of Spring in her nostrils that she died quietly and as far as could be seen without pain. We buried her under a lilac bush in the garden, and my wife replanted a great clump of primroses above where she lies to remind us of an agreeable cat, who might not have had much positive personality, but was always friendly; had the most beautiful green eyes; and was remarkable in that she was the only cat I ever knew who liked to walk at heel, would stop on order, and would wait patiently and obediently at the stopping-place until she was picked up again.

She seemed to prefer human beings to those of her own kind. She little knew!

V.G.